Praying for Miracles

Praying for Miracles

Exploring the Rational and Biblical Basis For Believing in a Wonder-Working God

COURTNEY DANIEL DABNEY

RESOURCE *Publications* • Eugene, Oregon

PRAYING FOR MIRACLES
Exploring the Rational and Biblical Basis For Believing in a Wonder-Working God

Copyright © 2012 Courtney Daniel Dabney. All rights reserved. Except for brief quotations in critical publications or reviews, no part of this book may be reproduced in any manner without prior written permission from the publisher. Write: Permissions, Wipf and Stock Publishers, 199 W. 8th Ave., Suite 3, Eugene, OR 97401.

Resource Publications
An Imprint of Wipf and Stock Publishers
199 W. 8th Ave., Suite 3
Eugene, OR 97401
www.wipfandstock.com

ISBN 13: 978-1-61097-997-9
Manufactured in the U.S.A.

All scripture quotations, unless otherwise indicated, taken from the New American Standard Bible®, Copyright © 1960, 1962, 1963, 1968, 1971, 1972, 1973, 1975, 1977, 1995 by The Lockman Foundation. Used by permission.

*To my husband Mark, whose love and support
allowed me to fulfill a dream in writing this book.
You are a constant reminder of God's miraculous redemption in my life.
To my daughter Allison, my son Jack, and my step-son Harrison,
may you continue to be amazed by your Savior
and witness His miraculous presence in your lives.*

Psalm 77:11–15

11I shall remember the deeds of the Lord;
Surely I will remember Your wonders of old.
12I will meditate on all Your work
And muse on Your deeds.
13Your way, O God, is holy;
What god is great like our God?
14You are the God who works wonders;
You have made known Your strength among the peoples.
15You have by Your power redeemed Your people,
The sons of Jacob and Joseph.

Contents

Preface ix

Section I   Why We Believe in a God of Miracles

  1   If God Exists, then Miracles Are Possible 3

  2   Miracles Are the Backbone of All World Religions 12

  3   Lies People Choose to Believe Instead 20

  4   How Big Is Your God? 29

Section II   Testing the Lord

  5   Testing Is Not Always A Bad Thing 39

  6   Isn't Praying for Miracles A Sin? 49

  7   Doesn't It Mean I Am An Immature Believer? 58

  8   Faithful or Faithless? 64

  9   God Honors Our Request for Fleeces 76

Section III   God's Communication Style

  10   God Chooses to Use Miracles, Signs, and Wonders 91

  11   The True Meaning of Faith 101

  12   How to Grow Your Mustard Seed 111

  13   Are Miracles Still Seen Today? 120

  14   Pray Big! 129

Bibliography 137

Preface

There once was a time when the occurrence of miracles was not in question. People used to have a healthy respect for an all-powerful God, and His ability to step into time and space and perform miracles. That is certainly not the case today. The pendulum has swung so far in the opposite direction, that people will do almost anything to distance themselves from the miracles, signs and wonders found in the Bible. Whether this discomfort with the miraculous takes the form of complacency, cowardice, or out-right combativeness, the church has had a difficult time standing her ground on the issue. I think the view of the evangelical church, regarding miracles, has been formed by forces both from without, as well as from within.

In the first section of the book, I take up two theories that have relegated miracles to the level of absurdity, or at the very least, to mere literary device. The first is the philosophy of humanism, and the second is the theory of evolution. Humanism, which seeks to elevate mankind, if not outright deify him, is a philosophy that is so pervasive that you hardly notice it anymore. The cultural exaltation of man, his achievements, and his seemingly limitless potential began in the Middle Ages, but really took root as a formal theory in the 1800's. Today its influence is everywhere you turn from political agendas, to educational systems, to advertising slogans.

We have been pickled in its brine from infancy, so much so, that we are hardly even aware of the imposing affect it has on our personal belief system. In essence, humanist philosophy makes God irrelevant. It states that mankind can fix his own problems and even develop utopian societies, with the aid of nothing outside of his rational mind, and certainly without any help from God. It also seems that rational thought has somehow become synonymous with scientific thought. Addressing these

Preface

unfortunate notions is the first step to recapturing a true understanding of Scriptures' teaching about miracles.

In our society, evolution is preached at every turn. Even though, as Bible-believing Christians, we don't accept what evolution espouses, I am afraid that we have made a little room for evolution in our theology. Without taking a long, hard look at this theory, and how far its reach has extended, we cannot regain a Biblical worldview, nor accurately defend against it. We have to understand how our culture has affected our belief system, before we can unravel how that belief system has affected our view of the miraculous, as well as our view of a wonder-working God.

We are so uncomfortable with miracles, that fear seems to have crept its way into our exposition of Scripture. In the second section of the book, I will take up a few examples of this. As Christians, our theology may have been influenced by outside forces, and our minds may have already been made up on the issue of miracles, before we ever open the Bible and study what it actually teaches on the subject. That is putting the cart before the horse, and not allowing the Scripture to speak for itself, but rather, imposing our already formed beliefs onto the Bible. It is a poor hermeneutic, and one which is sure to give us a faulty understanding of God's purposes for, as well as His uses of, miracles.

The fact of the matter is, that from the time of the Reformation, Protestants have felt a need to distance themselves from the miracles touted by the Catholic church. It was a time in history when the Catholic church was using miracles to validate its sole authority, as well as to subjugate the untrained masses, who at that time in history, had no access or ability to read the Bible for themselves. So, some of our Protestant discomfort with the miraculous can trace its roots all the way back to the 1500's.

In the evangelical church we are also responding, to some degree, to our Pentecostal brothers, who seem to place too great an emphasis on the book of Acts, and have formed their theology around the gifts of the Spirit. While we might be able to make a case that some of the Apostolic gifts given by the Holy Spirit in the early church (specifically tongues, prophesy, healing and miracles) may no longer be in use in this age, let's be careful not to infer that we are in another period of silence (like the 400 years that passed between the Testaments). My point is that reactionary theology is not sound theology either. Just because believers may not be supernaturally gifted to perform miracles or to heal people, like the Apostles and members of the early church were, does not mean that God does not perform miracles or heal the sick in our day and age. God is still at work in His church, and He still works miracles. We cannot allow our discomfort with the issue of miracles to taint our study of the Scriptures.

In the last section of the book we will take a look at some other issues that are crucial to our interaction with our wonder-working God. Without a right relationship to God, based on our acceptance of the free gift He offered us in salvation, praying for miracles is akin to rubbing a lucky rabbit's foot. I go into the subject of faith and the fact that faith, in and of itself, is utterly powerless. But God is power*ful*, and when we are plugged into the right source, we can see His miracles, signs and wonders vividly.

This book is the culmination of years of study on the subject. I have been convinced of the fact that God works in miraculous ways since I was nineteen years old, when I experienced His power first hand, during a mission trip to Germany. Many of these views took shape during my training at Dallas Theological Seminary. Over the years, it has saddened me to see how the church has distanced itself from God's awesome power, even buying into our culture's obvious disdain for miracles. God meant for His church to walk in power and experience His presence in its daily life. I think we have been pushed slightly off center, and it is my hope that this book will help you regain a firm footing on the subject of miracles, and prepare you to stand your ground when confronted with a culture, who neither believes in, nor worships our wonder working God.

SECTION I

Why We Believe in a God of Miracles

1

If God Exists, Then Miracles Are Possible

As Christians, we find ourselves far outside the mainstream when it comes to our belief in miracles. There are deeply entrenched philosophies and long-held theories that disregard God Himself and any notion of His wonders, which reside apart from the scientific arena. We have to begin our exploration of miracles, by first understanding why our culture is so opposed to them, and so quick to dismiss those of us who believe in a wonder-working God.

Christianity and miracles go hand in hand. One cannot exist without the other. This foundational belief in a God who performs miracles is counter-culture, especially in our modern, western society. In fact, our belief in miracles is one of the main reasons that non-believers discredit Christianity. They claim it is not scientific and therefore easily classified as mythology and lore.

Our rational culture teaches, from elementary school through university, that the world's major religions were simply a group of myths created by simple and uneducated ancient people. We are told that the crafters of the great civilizations of the ancient world were just a bunch of superstitious buffoons. The same people who laid the foundations for all that we know today—in the areas of art, literature, architecture, law, and philosophy—were just not advanced enough to grasp scientific thought. And because they were so intellectually stunted, they had no other option but to make up a fictitious God figure to worship.

This is one way modern men, sold out to humanistic philosophy and Darwinian theories, have simply dismissed the occurrence of miracles. They discount the miraculous on the basis of nothing more than the presumption that those who went before us didn't know as much as we do today. On that basis alone, they throw out miracles as antiquated notions and move on to *true knowledge*.

But, those same ancestors knew enough about the natural world, to know when to stand up and take notice. They were smart enough to know when God had intervened in their lives and performed a phenomenon otherwise unexplainable by natural means. They knew when a miracle had occurred. They knew that only something supernatural could change the course of otherwise natural events.

As C. S. Lewis in his ground-laying book *Miracles* pointed out:

> When a thing professes from the very outset to be a unique invasion of Nature by something from the outside, increasing knowledge of Nature can never make it either more or less credible than it was at the beginning. In this sense it is mere confusion of thought to suppose that advancing science has made it harder for us to accept miracles.[1]

But, that is precisely the faulty logic that permeates our institutions of higher learning. We live in a post-modern world. The anti-God movement of the late nineteenth century has become the accepted *truth* of today. Darwin proposed his theory which replaced our belief in a Creator God with the idea of evolution, and scientists, already steeped in humanism, latched onto it. (By the way, it is still Darwin's *theory* of evolution. It has never successfully been proven. It has never become Darwin's *fact* of evolution). Even though it is no more than any other man-made theory, evolution has been accepted and taught as if it were a scientific fact and proliferated to amazing degrees.

Philosophers of the day embraced this new evolutionary theory and added their voices. Although Friedrich Nietzsche proclaimed Him dead, and proposed an atheistic existence without Him, God's presence and impact are still seen powerfully today. Scholars, however, are still devoting their life's work to abolishing God from every sphere of academic enterprise and trying desperately to disprove His very existence. They toil over illogical rationalizations and never make any strides, because the evidence is so vastly opposing them. In other words, while Elvis may have left the building, God remains firmly seated on His throne. Psalm 14:1–3 states it this way:

---

1. Lewis, *Miracles*, 76.

*1*The fool has said in his heart, "There is no God."
They are corrupt, they have committed abominable deeds;
There is no one who does good.
*2*The Lord has looked down from heaven upon the sons of men
To see if there are any who understand, who seek after God.
*3*They have all turned aside, together they have become corrupt;
There is no one who does good, not even one.

Many of these modern scientists would also claim to be atheists. This became a very popular view and was embraced for decades by scholars in the early-mid 1900's, but its popularity and dogmatism have faded in recent decades. It is an intellectually untenable belief system. If God cannot be known, then how can you be *sure* He doesn't exist? How can you disprove a negative? Well, the answer is simple, unless you choose to plant yourself firmly on the side of dogmatic and irrational philosophy, you cannot.

The majority of American scientists today, however, would claim agnosticism over full-fledged atheism. It is a far more intellectual stance to be sure. Since, they believe, God's existence cannot be explored scientifically, they choose to remain reserved and say that *if* He does exist, they simply don't care. This, although very sad, at least shows a degree of rational and intellectual integrity. These folks may fight just as hard to discredit an all-powerful God, and elevate humanism and naturalism, but don't choose to do so under the label of atheism and thus hypocrisy.

One recent, and notable example of a scholar who made the switch from whole-hog atheist to confirmed agnostic is Dr. Richard Dawkins. The outspoken evolutionary biologist from Oxford University is antagonistic, to say the least, when referring to God and religious people in general. In fact on his website richarddawkins.net, his foundation proudly sells t-shirts printed with quotes from his book *The God Delusion*, like this one:

> The God of the Old Testament is arguably the most unpleasant character in all fiction: jealous and proud of it; a petty, unjust, unforgiving control-freak; a vindictive, bloodthirsty ethnic cleanser; a misogynistic, homophobic, racist, infanticidal, genocidal, filicidal, pestilential, megalomaniacal, sadomasochistic, capriciously malevolent bully.
> —Richard Dawkins, *The God Delusion*[2]

---

2. Richard Dawkins, "The God Delusion T-Shirt," Apparel.

Now that doesn't sound like an open-minded scientist to me. Can you even imagine walking around with that slogan printed on your t-shirt? How can someone who is so obviously angry, with what he believes to be a non-existent being, claim to have even a shred of impartiality in his scientific reasoning on the subject? I mean that seems like a lot of pent-up hostility directed toward an imaginary work of fiction. At any rate, after tirades like that in his writings and lectures over the past decades of his career, we learn that even Professor Dawkins would now prefer to be known as an agnostic, rather than labeled an outright atheist.

I won't spend any more time on atheism. You may still run into a few of these staunch atheists, typically well-tenured professors of our major universities, but their bias is so obvious, they simply cannot be taken seriously. To deny the existence of God outright, without any scientific evidence as a basis, goes against the very rules they choose to live by. Contradictions. Hypocrisy. Enough said.

This is what 2 Peter 2:17–19 says about this kind of thinking and teaching:

> [17]These are springs without water and mists driven by a storm, for whom the black darkness has been reserved.
> [18]For speaking out arrogant words of vanity they entice by fleshly desires, by sensuality, those who barely escape from the ones who live in error,
> [19]promising them freedom while they themselves are slaves of corruption; for by what a man is overcome, by this he is enslaved.

In this book, I obviously presume there is a God, because that is the only thing that makes any logical sense. The beauty and intricacy of the natural world, and of humanity itself, is too marvelous to have happened by random chance. To support such a belief system, would require mathematical and statistical gymnastics of Olympic proportions.

That is why the late Carl Sagan relied on *billions and billions of years* to explain his belief in the evolutionary hypothesis. Everyone agrees that in order for evolution to stand a fighting chance, you would actually need billions and billions of years to allow for even the potential of any type of evolutionary change within species, (much less for one species to *evolve* into another). He was so committed to the theory, that he concocted an explanation to allow for the distant possibility that it could be true.

To believe in randomness and chance is the definition of *blind faith*. Statistically speaking, Sagan didn't shoot far enough. Maybe he should have gone with *billions and trillions of years* to give evolutionists a little more running room. They'll need it! (The ever increasing number of zeros becomes necessary to distance the theory from the reality we actually find in nature). Sagan was leaning toward the trillion mark himself, in his book *Billions and Billions*:

> While the popularity of "Billions and Billions" has not entirely faded, these numbers too are becoming somewhat small-scale, narrow-visioned, and passé. A much more fashionable number in now on the horizon, or closer. The trillion is almost upon us.[3]

Let's get serious . . . Darwin's theory doesn't hold up to the scrutiny of even the youngest and most uneducated child. To believe that all we know came into being by accident is perhaps one of the greatest miracles to ever be posited, and the least scientific of all notions. Based upon all that we can observe and reason, life itself, as well as the natural order, simply scream for the existence of a Creator God, and for a rational, organized, and purposeful creation. Accidents, random chance and chaos do not magically create order, systems and seasons.

To suppose that such intricate design is the result of some *cosmic whoops* is too far-fetched to be believed (although somehow it is blindly accepted and taught as fact by learned men and women). Generations of our children have been force-fed this agenda to liberate man from a supreme being, in the name of science. How can a teacher or professor stand up with a straight face and tell their students that even though we have no observable evidence to offer as proof (turning rational thought into a mockery), and that even though it doesn't adhere to fundamental tenants of reason (turning philosophy into a mockery), and that even though it does not stand the test of the scientific method (making science itself a mockery), evolution should be believed nonetheless?

What happened to the missing link? If there was a point in time when apes transitioned or *evolved* into mankind, there should not be just one missing link they are clamoring for, but vast numbers of these imaginary creatures who made that giant leap. We should have found huge societies of them to offer up as evidence by now. It wouldn't be a needle in a haystack, now would it? A better question might be why *all* apes didn't

---

3. Sagan, *Billions and Billions*, 6.

become humans. Why are there still any apes at all? Since they failed to evolve like the rest of us, shouldn't they have become extinct by now?

Where did that incredibly dense matter come from, that somehow, and for some unknown reason, spontaneously exploded into the existence of everything we know? The laws of physics don't apply to a void of nothingness. If nothing existed, then nothing could expand. There had to be *something* in order for physics to ever come into play. For that matter, where did the space come from for the dense matter to explode into?

How do you get around the fact that everything observable actually proves a continual breakdown of form and function through time, and that species and natural orders actually deteriorate and degrade or *devolve* over time and not *evolve* into better and more sophisticated forms, which is crucial to the evolutionary scheme? We now have evidence that every time DNA is replicated, it is broken down and diluted a little bit more.

Adaptations within species (like thicker feathers in a colder climate) do not make the gigantic leap from one species to a completely different one, nor non-living matter to living matter. (Think Mary Shelley's Frankenstein!) Nothing inanimate has ever become alive. I don't care how many billions and trillions of zeros you add to the end of your equation. No scientist anywhere in the world can add a pinch of this, and a dash of that, and create life even as small as a single-celled organism. Every Petri dish in the world would sit vacant if not for something that was already deemed alive.

The recipe card for *life* simply doesn't exist. If we can't produce even a single cell of life from a non-living substance, with all our advanced technical expertise and scientific knowledge, then how can we be expected to believe that a single-celled organism, much less a brilliant multi-celled human being, ever managed to come into existence by some completely random chance? You expect me to believe that primordial soup coughed up life by churning together some random combination of ingredients, like that stew that was tasty but you can't duplicate it, because you forgot what you put in it?

Since those who espouse this fantastical view definitively refuse to believe in miracles, it seems they must believe in magic, because it would take a pretty big pile of pixie dust to achieve that scenario. There is no other logical explanation for mankind apart from a Creator. Psalm 139:13–16 says it this way:

> ^{13}For You formed my inward parts;
> You wove me in my mother's womb.
> ^{14}I will give thanks to You, for I am fearfully and wonderfully made;
> Wonderful are Your works,
> And my soul knows it very well.
> ^{15}My frame was not hidden from You,
> When I was made in secret,
> And skillfully wrought in the depths of the earth;
> ^{16}Your eyes have seen my unformed substance;
> And in Your book were all written
> The days that were ordained for me,
> When as yet there was not one of them.

To claim that things change over time is one thing. To claim that everything accidently came into being from so-called *primordial soup*, with life appearing out of a void, mysteriously and magically, and then continuing to improve into life as we know it, over the course of billions and billions of years is ridiculous. Yeah, there are just a few holes in the evolutionary theory! Never mind all that.

To be sure, the scientific community has taken a long detour (about 150 years long). But, unless a person of science chooses to continue on as a sheep, following the flock blindly, while putting their brain in neutral, the evidence for an intelligent designer is overwhelming. It cannot be missed! Believing in a supernatural designer does not make one less scientific. It just make them infinitely more original than their peers, who choose to follow rather than dare to buck the current establishment.

While on a recent trip to Carlsbad Caverns in New Mexico, our family went to watch the awe-inspiring sight of swirling bats as they exited the cave entrance on their nightly flight. The forest ranger said something amazing during her educational lecture about the bats. She stated that the oldest fossilized remains of any bat were some 52 million years old (based on carbon dating). She said that the scientists could not find any marked difference between that ancient bat and the bat species we find today. She stated clearly that the evidence proved that bats have not changed much at all over the past *52 million years*!

Then the Ranger added, and I quote, "That must mean . . . that bats evolved prior to 52 million years ago."

What?! Did she really say that? Instead of simply admitting that, at least in the case of bats, we have *no* scientific evidence of *any* type of evolution, she made the giant, and completely unsubstantiated leap, to claim that evolution was true, in rejection of all the scientific evidence placed before her, and stated that *therefore* bats had to evolve prior to the evidence we have obtained in the past 52 million years.

She, like so many other scientists, is completely sold out to evolution no matter what the evidence proves or where the logic leads. The overwhelming presupposition for them is that evolution equals scientific fact, no matter what the facts really are. By the way . . . no one else in the audience of over one hundred people, questioned her on her faulty reasoning, they just continued nodding their heads in agreement. "All we like sheep . . ."

THOUGHT QUESTIONS FOR CHAPTER 1

1. What are some ways that atheism and evolutionary theory have influenced our society?
2. How do you think it has affected things like: media, education, environmental issues, political agendas?
3. How has this philosophy pervaded our culture in the past 150 years?
4. How is your children's or grandchildren's education different from your own. In other words, how fast has this philosophy taken hold of our society?
5. Do you think this view of life and after-life has infected the church? If so, how?
6. Has it diminished our view of God and changed our feelings about miracles?

2

Miracles Are the Backbone of All World Religions

THE SCIENTIFIC AND POST-MODERNIST mentality, which is completely sold out to humanism and the evolutionary scheme, is vastly outnumbered. They make up only a tiny minority worldwide. They just have lofty platforms in Western institutions of higher education and the media from which to promulgate their view and tend to scream the loudest in order not to be drowned out.

Interestingly, a firm belief in a Creator God has not altogether been over-taken by humanism. The fact of His presence has not been *educated* out of us. There are billions of God-believers, of all faiths, throughout the world. Many of them have high IQ's and intellectual abilities. Both children and adults believe that God can interact with His creation, and that miracles are not only possible, but probable.

People everywhere believe in miracles. This notion is innate to all humanity and God put that belief within us. This belief in the miraculous transcends all cultural and religious boundaries. In fact, without miracles none of the world's major religions would exist. That's right—Buddhism, Hinduism, Islam, Judaism, and Christianity all have the miraculous at their very core.

The most popular religious form in our current American culture, for instance, relies upon the miraculous, though they might prefer to call it mysticism. New Age teachings talk about the god in us. They put human beings on par with God, so we can all be our own god and make up our own rules. New Agers borrow these philosophical ideas from Buddhism

Miracles Are the Backbone of All World Religions

and Hinduism and their teachings about the god within. In all three of these religions, the ultimate goal is to attain Nirvana and become *self-actualized* enough to become a drop in the vast god-ocean, where a soul becomes a part of this god. On one's journey to this wonderful place, the individual can gauge their personal progress by their ability to actually perform miracles, to do things outside of the natural realm.

New Agers believe that the further they progress in their journey (which often takes several lifetimes) they will be capable of clairvoyance, astral projection, be able to have knowledge of their previous lives, and even levitate. In the ancient writings of both Buddhism and Hinduism, we find times where the god's (they have many deities, with different names and particular character traits) take on human form and perform miracles among us. So, miracles play a crucial role in Buddhism, and Hinduism, as well as all New Age off-shoots of the two.

Islam holds that the prophet Mohammed was transported in his night journeys. The Qur'an would never have been written unless Mohammed believed in the visions he witnessed on these miraculous journeys. It was precisely the miraculous nature of these reported events that lent credibility to the writings, and that is why they are held so fiercely today. There is also the much heralded miracle of Muhammad splitting the moon in half. By miraculous encounters like these, the prophet Muhammad proved himself to be a prophet to his followers. What faithful Muslims and Islamic adherents practice and teach are intricately linked to miracles. The Muslim faith would not exist apart from the miraculous.

Judaism, from which Christianity obviously derives its heritage, is rooted in the miraculous. God proves Himself to be the one true God, and displays His power through miracles, signs and wonders. The ministries of key leaders and patriarchs, the prophets, as well as the Messiah Himself, are all authenticated by miracles. In both religions the supernatural is a necessary component. Since they both believe in one deity, they insist upon His ability to act like God and do things that human beings are incapable of doing or explaining. Therefore, in Jewish and Christian texts, God proves Himself to be God by miracles, signs, and wonders.

So, we find that God and His miraculous abilities are at the core of thinking and believing people everywhere. To dismiss people as intellectual pigmies, based upon their belief in such a God, is outrageously unfair and inherently prejudiced. That's right, I said *prejudiced*! It is especially offensive to categorize all believer's in God (and particularly Christians it seems in recent decades) as ignorant or misguided. The billions of people of all these faiths worldwide cannot all be classified as delusional, uneducated, and misinformed. There are simply too many of us to discount as idiots.

All those who seek to discredit God fail to understand the basis of wisdom. Proverbs 1:5–7 explains where to find true wisdom:

> [5]A wise man will hear and increase in learning,
> And a man of understanding will acquire wise counsel,
> [6]To understand a proverb and a figure,
> The words of the wise and their riddles.
> [7]The fear of the LORD is the beginning of knowledge;
> Fools despise wisdom and instruction.

Yet, this has become the accepted norm by the scholastic, and their close friends the media. They get up on soap-boxes and piously preach the value of diversity and tolerance. How can you dismiss God-believing people like me as unwitting fools, who simply lack exposure to some unique insight and education? What happened to *coexisting*?

Believing peoples of every faith are part of the very *diversity* they proclaim to be so necessary and desirable for modern society. But, on closer inspection, what they really advocate is their own brand of diversity. They really mean to include only those people and philosophies they deem desirable and who are in agreement with their own forms of morality and politics. That is the *so-called diversity* they choose to protect.

In this politically correct world, positively anything goes, anything can be tolerated, except for any type of religion where there might be a Creator God to stand in judgment of them. Diversity and tolerance are only trotted out to praise those in agreement with the powers that be, and also used to punish anyone with opposing views. I think it would be far more accurate to characterize what they value as *total homogeneity*, since they only value like-minded fellows. Yet, people of faith vastly outnumber the ranks of the faithless. Nietzsche couldn't kill Him by proclaiming Him dead, and God is still very much alive and well.

Ephesians 5:6–13 warns us in regards to people who try to deceive us with their words:

> [6]Let no one deceive you with empty words, for because of these things the wrath of God comes upon the sons of disobedience.
> [7]Therefore do not be partakers with them;

> ⁸for you were formerly darkness, but now you are Light in the Lord; walk as children of Light
> ⁹(for the fruit of the Light *consists* in all goodness and righteousness and truth),
> ¹⁰trying to learn what is pleasing to the Lord.
> ¹¹Do not participate in the unfruitful deeds of darkness, but instead even expose them;
> ¹²for it is disgraceful even to speak of the things which are done by them in secret.
> ¹³But all things become visible when they are exposed by the light, for everything that becomes visible is light.

So, atheism is a relic of the post-modern age. It is inconsistent with observable fact and rational thought, and blatantly contradicts the scientific method it claims to live by. Evolution, as well, is a modern myth and no more scientific than any other unproven theory.

I don't care how many scientists stand on the side of evolution. As you may recall, at one time in history, all the scientists in the known world believed that the Earth was flat. They were all wrong too! And their near unanimous consensus about that untruth could not make it any more true. In the same way, the current deafening chant among the modern day scientific community does not and cannot make evolutionary theory into a fact. No amount of faith and trust and pixie dust, no amount of zeros added to the end of the equation, can make it true.

Many scholars, scientists and lawyers have struck out on a quest to disprove the existence of the God of the Bible. Many have been converted in the process of their open-minded research. Physicist Hugh Ross, wrote an eloquent piece entitled *Why I Believe in the Miracle of Divine Creation*. In it, he summed up his argument this way:

> The community of believers has no reason to fear and every reason to anticipate the advance of scientific research into the origin and characteristics of the cosmos. The more we learn the more evidence we accumulate for the existence of God and for his identity as the God revealed in the Bible. Those who fight hardest against a supernatural, or theistic, explanation for the cosmos often produce the most powerful new evidence for it. As technology produces new measuring tools and theoretical capacities increase, the clearer the case for Christ the Creator will grow.[1]

---

1. Ross, "Miracle of Divine Creation," 157.

I would also like to point out that everyone holds some form of belief-system. Whether you align yourself with one of the major world religions, some type of cult, a belief in non-belief like atheism or agnosticism, a faith in the natural world above all else, as in Naturalism, or atheism plus some form of ethics and morality, as in the newly minted Secular Humanism, you hold certain beliefs to be true while rejecting others. You have a faith, you have a religion, and you have a belief-system.

According to the Council for Secular Humanism website they incorrectly define themselves as nonreligious, they state:

> Secular humanism is *nonreligious*, espousing no belief in a realm or beings imagined to transcend ordinary experience. Secular humanists see themselves as undesigned, unintended beings who arose through evolution, possessing unique attributes of self-awareness and moral agency.[2]

They state that they are both evolutionists, and self-aware moralists. Those are matters of faith. In fact, Webster's Dictionary defines *religious* this way: "relating to or manifesting faithful devotion to an acknowledged ultimate reality or deity."[3] Although they adamantly deny the deity part, their Secular Humanism clearly manifests faithful devotion to an acknowledged ultimate reality. By definition they are not *nonreligious* as they claim, but hold to a particular brand of religion, with a very well-defined set of beliefs.

Everyone has a belief system, everyone holds to faith in their views of ultimate reality. Even if your faith or your religion choose not to credit or acknowledge God, you are a *believer* in some belief system. Even though Secular Humanism tries to distance itself from all forms of accepted *religion,* it is itself a religion.

And, while we're on the subject . . . I have one more question for Secular Humanists. Where did your so-called *moral agency* come from? Morality does not evolve! Darwin's theory of evolution has a very difficult time dealing with the obvious contradiction of human morality. Having left this glaring issue dangling in his *The Origin of Species*, Darwin has to confront it and try to make man's morality somehow fit into his new scheme. So, he wrote the *Descent of Man* in that effort. Even though *The Origin of Species* laid out evolution, and his theory of survival of the fittest

2. Kurtz, "Secular Humanist Manifesto 2000."
3. Merriman Webster Dictionary Online, "Religious."

in great detail, the morality of man and civilized society do not fit into the evolutionary scheme, and in fact, contradict it outright. So there has to be something different about mankind (who Darwin refers to as *higher animals* versus all other less evolved species or *lower animals*). I do not have time to give full attention to this idea in a book of this scope, but feel free to amuse yourself by reading chapter five of Darwin's *Descent of Man*, in which he tries desperately to make sense of the issue.

He goes on and on dancing around this *real* problem for his theory, and trying to convince his reader of how tribes developed self-sacrificial values for the good of the entire tribe, leading to the greater success of the society. When in fact the more vicious savages, those who literally ate up the competition, tended to fair far better than the more benevolent tribes throughout history. Reference Teddy Roosevelt's most famous quote on diplomacy, "Speak softly and carry a big stick," which was actually taken from an old African proverb. No matter how Darwin dances around it, the fact is that the more proficient a society is at war, the greater success tends to come to that group. Unfortunately, it is not always the group with the highest set of morals that wins the day.

This is Darwin's only option though, since he has to admit that natural selection cannot possibly account for the morality of men. There has to be something outside the theory of evolution to explain it. In fact the whole idea of survival of the fittest denounces morality outright. The need for animals to eat or be eaten for their own survival does not magically morph into human morality. And while the very idea of morality obviously did not come from evolution, it did come from somewhere. Perhaps it was endowed to mankind by a Creator God with a true moral compass. Secular Humanists should open their minds for a minute, and really question that fact rather than blindly agreeing with their errant manifesto.

Human morality is inherent in mankind because man was created in the image of God. Let's follow the logic where it leads and not skirt the issue because it is more convenient for us. Left to rules of evolution, mankind would logically lead toward anarchy and immorality in a kind of Wild West, every man for himself scenario, the fittest trampling under foot those less equipped. Without a Creator God, our society's moral structures simply make no sense. And yet, we find morality at the core of every human civilization. You simply cannot use the argument of evolution when it suits you (to dismiss the presence God), and then ignore it, or outright contradict it, when it does not (stating your *morality* as a key component of your faith).

As we have seen the world is populated with billions of God-fearing people, who should have, according to evolutionary theory, died out with the likes of prehistoric dinosaurs or medieval dragons. The dawn of scientific thought and reason should have put an end to all world religions as men became more educated and self-aware. But, we find that atheists, agnostics and secular humanists are not the only logical-minded, educated and scientific people on the face of the Earth. In other words, it is possible to have a brain and also believe in a Creator God, and in His miraculous nature, as the members of all major world religions do, including Christians. It is the height of arrogance to dismiss all of us outright, on the basis of nothing more than a distaste for our flavor of diversity.

THOUGHT QUESTIONS FOR CHAPTER 2

1. In what ways do you feel your Christian faith has been side-lined or discounted by those who choose to believe in evolution, or humanistic philosophies?
2. How has the educational system added to the pervasive attitude that Christianity, as well as all religions, are simply uneducated or superstitious?
3. Do you feel the media has contributed to dismissing religious peoples of all faiths? Specifically of Christians?
4. What part does political correctness play in this, including terms like tolerance and diversity?
5. Did you realize that Christians are among the majority in their belief in a Creator God, rather than the minority as we are often made to feel?
6. Why do illogical schemes such as Secular Humanism get a pass on their logic and rhetoric, while Christianity seems to be scrutinized and even persecuted?

3

Lies People Choose to Believe Instead

THERE ARE A FEW more hurdles people have to believing in a God of miracles. One of the biggest that we will take on in this chapter is exaltation of self, or pride. It is a tough hurdle to overcome and one of the main things that stands in the way of many unsaved people.

Since there is a God, then by nature, He must be all-together superior to us. If we are talking about God with all His attributes and qualities, He would have to be completely superior to mankind, or else He would not be God at all. If I, myself, can become Him (as some believe) or if I am a little piece of Him (a drop in His ocean) then He is not unique and does not qualify to be called God. As I mentioned earlier, New Age religions as well as Hinduism and Buddhism, see mankind as perfecting over the course of several lifetimes, with the ultimate destination to become like or a part of God.

But, by necessity, God must be superior in every respect to me. To believe that, only takes a logical mind, but to accept that, takes remarkable humility. If God is truly God, then He must be capable of altering the typical or standard way in which His creation operates. He must be capable of the miraculous, or else He is no different than man, bound by time, matter, and scientific processes. If He is bound by His creation then He is disqualified from ruling over it. Therefore a belief in God and a belief in His ability to perform miracles go hand in hand. And, an awesome Creator God like that deserves our unwavering devotion and worship!

To deny the existence of the all-powerful deity is inexcusable. But people do it every day. Some go to extremes to deny Him and make

Lies People Choose to Believe Instead

up elaborate lies to dismiss Him. It is obvious that God exists. Romans 1:18–20 explains this eloquently:

> [18] For the wrath of God is revealed from heaven against all ungodliness and unrighteousness of men who suppress the truth in unrighteousness,
> [19] because that which is known about God is evident within them; for God made it evident to them.
> [20] For since the creation of the world His invisible attributes, His eternal power and divine nature, have been clearly seen, being understood through what has been made, so that they are without excuse.

Since He exists, miracles are possible. An all-powerful God is the only explanation that makes sense of our world. Billions of people of faith around the world agree and desire to know Him. But, in the absence of that, or in an effort to forcefully deny that He exists, people will cling to any cult, theory or philosophy they can dream up.

A few years back on a trip to Seattle, Washington a friend and I were amazed to find so many outrageous religious offerings. Ideas that would not gain a single follower in one part of the country, seem to flourish in others. On a stroll down one mostly residential street, we came across many options: Celtic reconstructionist paganism, a college for astrological arts and sciences, Earth Ministry—which tries to connect their followers to the earth, and one spiritual group who claimed to hear the whales through telepathic animal communicators. I am not kidding! It is all out there just take your pick—and you can wash it all down with a little primordial soup while you're at it. Do they really think the Bible is so far-fetched that they would rather latch on to some of these concoctions instead?

Unfortunately Thomas Jefferson, our beloved founding father is another sad example. Have you ever heard of the Jefferson Bible? In it you will find no mention of the supernatural or anything miraculous. Thomas Jefferson created his own personal version of the Bible, by taking out all references to miracles or anything which could not be explained *scientifically*. With scissors in hand, Jefferson compiled a cut and paste version of the four Gospels. He intentionally extracted all supernatural references. Interestingly, he never allowed this version of the Bible to be printed during his lifetime. It would have caused quite a stir.

In his *Life and Morals of Jesus of Nazareth*, Jefferson had hoped to present only Jesus' teachings as a moral and ethical code to emulate. To him the Scripture was merely an ancient compilation of morals and ethics. No power. No miracles. No hope. Can you even imagine the Gospels without them? That is what Thomas Jefferson set out to present. His version ends this way:

> Now, in the place where he was crucified, there was a garden; and in the garden a new sepulcher, wherein was never a man yet laid. There laid they Jesus. And rolled a great stone to the door of the sepulcher, and departed.[1]

That's it! End of the story! No mention of a resurrection. Jesus just laid there and rotted. How very sad. So, how do we answer the popular question . . . was Thomas Jefferson a Christian? Well, if he believed in his version of Scripture, I'm sorry to say, he was not. Without resurrection there is no hope of salvation. And, of course, without miracles there is no resurrection from the dead.

There are a few major details that Jefferson (or anyone like him) overlooks by removing all miracles from a version of the Gospel accounts. You cannot have a moral, ethical, or philosophical triumph, by a man who *claimed* to be God and was therefore a total and complete liar. Being a liar, and even one of world-renown, never makes it to the top of anyone's moral, ethical or philosophical to-do list. Liars are rarely invited to partake in those kinds of debates and never receive such accolades. Jesus Christ claimed to be the Son of God. If He was lying about it, that seems to be a glaring problem for a moral giant, as Jefferson thought Him to be. Reference Matthew 16:13–17 where we find:

> [13]Now when Jesus came into the district of Caesarea Philippi, He was asking His disciples, "Who do people say that the Son of Man is?"
> [14]And they said, "Some say John the Baptist; and others, Elijah; but still others, Jeremiah, or one of the prophets."
> [15]He said to them, "But who do you say that I am?"
> [16]Simon Peter answered, "You are the Christ, the Son of the living God."
> [17]And Jesus said to him, "Blessed are you, Simon Barjona, because flesh and blood did not reveal this to you, but My Father who is in heaven."

---

1. Jefferson, *The Jefferson Bible*, 168.

The claim to be the Messiah and the Son of the living God is insurmountable. You can't simply ignore it away. If you deny that claim, yet admire and choose to emulate the man, you do so at your own intellectual and spiritual peril. I would like to add another quote by C. S. Lewis on the subject. In his book *Miracles,* he states this regarding Jesus:

> The discrepancy between the depth and sanity and (let me add) *shrewdness* of His moral teaching and the rampant megalomania which must lie behind His theological teaching unless He is indeed God, has never been satisfactorily got over.[2]

This is a brilliant point, because if *all* that Christ said and did are not entirely true, then really *everything* about Him would sum up to nothing more than a huge contradiction.

The other gaping hole in this kind of endeavor, to extract anything unexplainable or miraculous, is that Christ stated His purpose as that of salvation not merely becoming a great moral teacher to emulate. John 11:24–27 says:

> [24]Martha said to Him, "I know that he will rise again in the resurrection on the last day."
> [25]Jesus said to her, "I am the resurrection and the life; he who believes in Me will live even if he dies,
> [26]and everyone who lives and believes in Me will never die. Do you believe this?"
> [27]She said to Him, "Yes, Lord; I have believed that You are the Christ, the Son of God, even He who comes into the world."

He did not teach, preach and perform miracles, merely to leave behind an outstanding moral code for others to emulate. If Jesus had merely wanted to impart good morals or ethics, he could have spared Himself the horrific death by crucifixion. What was the purpose of all that? Why get on the wrong side of the religious establishment and get yourself tortured and killed by claiming to be God? How does that serve the purpose of a philosopher and ethicist? That kind of behavior doesn't make someone more philosophical, or ethical, it simply makes them more of a lunatic.

As ridiculous as that sounds, many current theologians and philosophers are still taking a pair of scissors to the Scripture in their attempts to make Jesus more benign and his ministry more palatable to today's highly

---

2. Lewis, *Miracles*, 174.

educated and skeptical masses. What they are really opposed to are all the miracles.

The recent Jesus Seminar is a perfect example. A group of liberal theologians sat down together in 1993 and voted amongst themselves which things they thought Jesus actually said and did during his ministry. If a particular passage did not get enough votes, they simply dismissed it as non-historical and irrelevant. They believed themselves and our modern culture to be far too sophisticated to fall for all that old-time religion stuff. These scholars thought that only those crazy fundamentalists actually believe in that supernatural nonsense anymore. While they feel more capable of true understanding, and choose to live without *irrational* miracles.

Well, unfortunately the Bible does not give anyone that luxury. If you cut out any portion of it, the whole house of cards falls around your feet. Miracles are not something we have to somehow *get around* or make excuses for. They are, quite literally, the crux of the story. Without miracles, there is no story. If we choose to leave Christ, a mere man, to rot in His tomb, and do not allow for God to be God, and raise Him from the dead, then the rest is no more than just words on a page, utterly meaningless to inform our moral lives in any respect. More importantly, if there are no miracles, and Christ never died to pay the price for our sin, and never rose from the dead, then we are as hopeless and helpless as ever. Without salvation and hope what good is living a moral life anyway.

Without miracles we are doomed to live our lives and our eternities apart from God. As the Apostle Paul concluded in I Corinthians 15:16–19:

> [16]For if the dead are not raised, not even Christ has been raised;
> [17]and if Christ has not been raised, your faith is worthless; you are still in your sins.
> [18]Then those also who have fallen asleep in Christ have perished.
> [19]If we have hoped in Christ in this life only, we are of all men most to be pitied.

Theologians and philosophers who choose to limit God and take away His ability to do anything outside the natural order are satisfied to rest their lives and eternal destinies upon the scientific method and their own rational and intellectual abilities. But, it doesn't take a rocket scientist to know that everyone has their limitations. How arrogant to be unwilling

Lies People Choose to Believe Instead

to allow for the possibility that someone (like God) might know something that you don't.

For example, my husband is an architect. I am not an architect. I know I have a sharp mind and am capable of many things, but designing buildings is not on that list. Don't ask me to design you a building. You wouldn't like the outcome. I am well aware of my limitations and quite sure I don't know everything. What these scholars all lack is humility. They cannot make room for a deity or any kind of supreme knowledge or supreme power. That would make them feel too inferior. Maybe you know someone who cannot find a way around their own ego long enough to meet their Savior. Maybe you recall being trapped in that same rut yourself.

While we are on the subject, let's explore the scientific method for a moment. According to the scientific method, only that which is repeatable can be known for sure. Repeatability is paramount for the process of observation. Well that excludes all of history, because none of it can be repeated. So, based upon that logic, nothing that has happened in the past can be truly known and it all remains up for debate making all of human history totally subjective.

For instance, I once had a long discussion with a neo-Nazi skin-head who, even after being shown footage of Holocaust survivors being liberated from concentration camps by Allied soldiers, as they walked past mass graves, claimed it was all a hoax and just a propaganda film created by the Jews. You can't argue with that kind of willful ignorance any more than offering light to a blind man. For some people history is completely subjective.

That also excludes evolution as a scientific endeavor, since no evolving (from one kind into a complete other kind) has ever been observed, nor can it be without the lapse of billions or trillions of years. The fossil record has failed to provide even one example of linking the *evolution* of one species to another by a *transitional* form. The few fossils that evolutionist point to could have legitimately been a known species that is simply now extinct, or could be a deformation of a known species rather than a mutation en route to a totally different form. We will never know, since only one random fossil is found at a time. If it is not repeatable you cannot ever prove it, nor can you disprove it scientifically.

That would seem to exclude miracles as well. If by definition, science requires the repeatable observation of an event, to prove or disprove a theory, and since, by definition, a miracle is a unique and unrepeatable event that happens counter to what we typically observe in nature, then science can neither prove nor can it disprove the occurrence of miracles.

It also excludes personal experience outright. Science excludes all experiential knowledge, unless it can be repeated, to prove it wasn't a fluke the first time around. Nevertheless, we learn an awful lot through our five senses. We learn valuable things like, riding our bike down-hill too fast on a gravel road, is unwise. And, even though we may not choose to repeat that foolish enterprise for the sake of science, we have still gained valuable knowledge and will do things differently to avoid the collision next time. My point is this: wisdom comes from many sources and not all of it is scientific. In other words, science is not the only basis for truth. Can't you just hear the collective scholastic gasp at that statement?

Charles Swindoll attacks the stance of those who dismiss God's miracles out of convenience, taking a slightly satirical tone in his book, *Growing Strong in the Seasons of Life*:

> Then what about miracles? Well, let's limit them to a child's world of fiction and fables. And, if necessary, to stained glass sanctuaries where emotion runs high and imagination is needed to make all those stories interesting. After all, what's a little religion without a pocketful of miracles? And if we started trying to account for all those things in the Bible, think of the time it would take to explain stuff like how the sun stood still, or why all those fish filled the disciples' nets, or what brought Lazarus back from beyond, or why Jesus' body has never been found, or how the death of Christ cleans up lives year after year, or how come the Bible is still around.
>
> Smart, keen-thinking skeptics don't have to worry about explaining little things like that. It's easier to simply embrace a wholesale denial of the miraculous . . . which is fine and dandy . . . until they themselves get sick, face death, and need miraculous help crossing that final river.[3]

So true! Nothing will improve your prayer life or change your view of God and His miracles like needing one for yourself. Let's face it, it is human nature to believe in something greater than ourselves. We choose to believe there is something capable of rising above the natural realm. It is the hardened heart of mankind that seeks to set aside the logical necessity

---

3. Swindoll, *Growing Strong in the Seasons of Life*, 102.

of an all powerful Creator God, or to imagine Him with His hands tied behind his back, unable or just unwilling to intervene.

At some point in everyone's life they are forced to either believe in God or reject their knowledge of Him in favor of a lie. Everyone who has faith in anything holds that faith, based upon their experiences. Scientists call that, empirical evidence. Whatever you call it, the existence of a Supreme Being cannot be denied, at least not with any intellectual credibility. In short, it takes more faith to believe that our intricate universe came into being on its own and by some random accident, than to simply and *humbly* acknowledge the existence of its awesome Creator.

THOUGHT QUESTIONS FOR CHAPTER 3

1. What kinds of lies did you believe before becoming a Christian?
2. Why is it so tempting to take a pair of scissors to Scripture and remove the parts you are uncomfortable with? Have you ever done that, just chosen to ignore truth because it was uncomfortable?
3. Have you ever chosen not to believe portions of Scripture because it took too much faith?
4. Did you at one time claim, or do you know someone who has claimed, that Jesus was a good teacher, while ignoring His claim to deity?
5. Why do you think the Jesus Seminar is appealing to people?
6. What part does humility play in salvation?

4

How Big Is Your God?

So, based on what we have seen, the existence of God is not in question. The question is whether God is really *God*. Can He work miracles? As we have already established, if He is not capable of doing anything out of the ordinary, then He is not qualified to be God. If your *god* cannot work miracles he is no *God* at all. He is nothing more than a mythological weakling, or an impotent fantasy.

We will examine this fact more closely in a future chapter when we study Ezekiel versus the prophets of Baal. This is the lesson God teaches to both Israel and the worshippers of the idol Baal. God proves Himself to be who He claims to be. In other words, if God created the natural order, He alone can transcend it.

If you agree that He is as awesome as Scriptures proclaim Him to be, then a bigger question remains. Are you willing to *allow* Him to be God? That takes humility. It requires you to get up off the throne and step aside, letting God take His rightful place. As we have already discovered, salvation itself requires a healthy dose of humility. To let go of all your personal striving to please God based upon your efforts and your own works, and admit your need for a Savior to do *all* the work for you, takes real humility. But, Salvation cannot be achieved apart from it. Having a proper view of yourself and your humanity is a stumbling block for many. It has become a very effective road block to salvation.

Most twelve step recovery programs are predicated on this one, all-important, realization. There is a higher power. There is no salvation, nor any healing without that understanding and without the necessary

Praying for Miracles

humility to bow your head. There is no basis for faith or belief without it. You cannot become a Christian without it. You must realize your humanity and recognize, revere and hold God in awe.

Only when you comprehend how utterly helpless, hopeless, and sinful you are as man, can you truly grasp how magnificent, outrageous, and powerful God's grace truly is. It's been said that you have to get someone good and lost before you can get them saved. That is so true! There is a reason people weep and fall to their knees when they come to Salvation. It is a powerful experience to be that humbled by your own humanity and overwhelming need, as well as, that amazed by God's provision and offer of grace.

The writer of Hebrews states it so clearly in chapter 2 verses 2–4:

> ²For if the word spoken through angels proved unalterable, and every transgression and disobedience received a just penalty,
> ³how will we escape if we neglect so great a salvation? After it was at the first spoken through the Lord, it was confirmed to us by those who heard,
> ⁴God also testifying with them, both by signs and wonders and by various miracles and by gifts of the Holy Spirit according to His own will.

God chooses to disclose Himself by signs and wonders and various miracles. He chooses to do amazing things to grow the faith of believers and authenticate Himself as the one true God, as He has done throughout history. I trust you have experienced that amazing grace for yourself.

Many Christians, even from lofty pulpits, and many with impressive degrees, teach that praying for miracles is faulty theology. They say that only the weak of faith or the immature, spiritually stunted, believer would ever do such a thing. They lambast the Apostle Thomas for his doubting and portray him to be some kind of hundred pound spiritual weakling, whose request for proof of the Lord's resurrection should be taken as a lesson to us all of what not to do. We'll explore that misconception in great detail.

They side-line Gideon's ministry because of his fleeces, stating that he was a lily-livered scaredy-cat, who should have been willing to simply obey and trust. They say he should never have asked for those fleeces and nor should you. They claim that praying for God to perform a miracle is tantamount to *testing* Him. But, they take the whole discourse out of context. In the following chapters, I will take up several of these long-held stereotypes and challenge them to the core. I think you'll find that asking God for miracles is not always a sign of immaturity and weakness—it is often exactly what is called for, and an embodiment of incredible faith.

Perhaps you don't ask big things of God, because deep down you don't expect He *can* and *will* answer big prayers. Deep down you think it is safer not to ask at all than to ask and be disappointed. Maybe your view of God is too small. Perhaps you don't pray for miracles because your faith is too weak. Maybe it takes a much deeper faith to step out of the way and watch God do wondrous things in your sight. Or possibly, it is just more convenient to deal with God on paper, and from a comfortable distance, than to witness Him up close and personally, and actually experience His power first-hand.

At this juncture, I feel the need to insert my personal testimony. I believe in miracles, not only because they are the backbone of Scripture and God chose to tell His story with them and through them, but because I have personally experienced miracles in my own life. I believe that God can do great things because I have witnessed His miraculous power myself.

The writers of Scripture did not shy away from the miracles they had seen. They were not ashamed to believe in miracles. They all attested to them and relayed them to their readers as what they had personally witnessed and beheld with their own eyes. So, I will do the same and explain what I have personally witnessed.

While I was saved in every literal sense at the age of seven, I didn't really comprehend the magnitude of *grace* until I was nineteen. I clearly understood my sin, and my need for a Savior to take my place and receive the punishment that I was due. I accepted that gift whole-heartedly when I was a child, and grew in my relationship to the Lord.

But, when I was seven years old, let's face it, I had not really experienced how sin separates you from the Lord. I had no real understanding or appreciation for how significant grace is, or how much it can cover. During my high school years, I played and made many mistakes, and the weight of my sin began to draw me away from the Lord. I longed for that relationship to be restored again. I began, as so many of us do, holding my sin against myself, in essence doing Satan's work for him. Its weight became an overwhelming burden. Maybe you have a similar story.

The truth was that my sins were already forgiven. All I had to do to restore fellowship was to confess them and move on. I John 1:9 says:

> ⁹If we confess our sins, He is faithful and righteous to forgive us our sins and to cleanse us from all unrighteousness.

But, Satan loves to get us caught in the trap of guilt and shame. Every time I made an attempt at restoring my fellowship with the Lord, he kept tapping me on the shoulder, and reminding me of my sin. And, I felt far from God.

During that time, I fell into one of the other most common pitfalls in the Christian life. I began to try to *be* good enough to please God on my own. Entire books in the New Testament (Galatians, Ephesians and Hebrews to name a few) are devoted to teaching believers how not to fall back into this tempting trap.

Now, this was not a conscious effort on my part, and had I stopped to analyze and put my actions into words, I would have seen the error of my ways. It is very tempting to pull yourself up by your bootstraps, and *be* a better person to gain acceptance in God's eyes. (So common, in fact, that every other major world religion is based entirely upon human effort and satisfying God solely on the good works of men.) Had you ever thought about that? Every other religion is based on what man does or does not do. Only Biblical Christianity is based on what God has done and will do. Human effort plays no role.

My senior year of high school, I began having extreme headaches. Tylenol would not touch them. The pain was so severe that I could not stand any movement, sound or light. The headaches made me nauseous and were exhausting. I had developed migraine headaches. My physician diagnosed these and gave me some pretty sobering news. According to his training, migraines are a lifelong ailment with no known cure. There were several possible triggers that I could learn to avoid, like red wine or strong cheese, but I would have to learn to manage my life with them from that point on.

The pain was so excruciating that tranquilizers had to be prescribed to numb it. My doctor also prescribed anti-depressants to, hopefully, minimize the frequency of the migraines. Without the anti-depressants, I was having a migraine every day and I was completely incapacitated. With the anti-depressants, I felt fuzzy-headed and a little loopy until about noon. When I got a migraine, still about one per week, I would have to leave work, or school or wherever and get home immediately. Then I would take a tranquilizer and, literally, knock myself out for eight hours. The tranquilizers took away the pain, but also a huge chunk of my life.

This was a very difficult way to live. I never knew when a migraine would take me out. But, I got used to my new lifestyle and tried to make the best of it. I actually thought I deserved it and took the burden on like some form of punishment for my sin. After all, as Satan continually pointed out . . . how could God ever want to be close to me? How could He ever forgive me? I could not fathom that kind of grace. So, I assumed that these migraines were some form of punishment, the natural consequence of sin in my life.

I went about my business, trying to *be* good enough to please God. I worked really hard at it, too. I was busily working part-time in college, taking unbelievable course loads, and maintaining my Dean's List honors. I had taken summer school religiously every summer, and was on pace to graduate in three years time. Why I put that kind of pressure on myself, I will never know.

Finally the summer between my junior and senior years, I simply had to take a break. I had finally reached burn-out. I was so stressed-out from over-achieving, and so tired of managing my life and my migraines, that I decided to take the summer off. My father had heard about a mission opportunity in Europe, and thought that a work crew assignment and evangelism might be just what I needed.

I went to Germany to a tiny village called Seeheim to work at a Bible School run by Greater Europe Mission. It was perfect, I could practice the language I had chosen to study throughout high school and college, travel and relax a bit doing mostly mindless odd jobs around the school. I picked cherries in a cherry orchard for days on end, caulked and painted a bathroom by myself, cut new room numbers out with a jigsaw, did laundry, cleaned toilets, cooked in the kitchen, and made countless beds. I had nothing but solitary time to assess my life and spend quiet time with the Lord.

While I was there, I did some sight-seeing and made some fabulous friends. One of them was the friend of a missionary couple at the Bible School. He was a German guitarist, and about a decade my senior. He truly believed in the power of prayer and had a unique closeness to the Lord. I learned a lot from him about God, His power, and how I could experience more of Him in my life. He really challenged me to grow.

During some of my quiet times and personal Bible studies, I studied through the Gospel of John. I was stopped dead in my tracks when I got to John 19:30:

> [30]Therefore when Jesus had received the sour wine, He said, "It is finished!" And He bowed His head and gave up His spirit.

If Christ said it was finished, then why was I still holding my sin over my own head? Why was I living a regretful life rather than the triumphant one He wanted for me? That's what grace meant. The debt for my sin had been paid in full. It was finished! Really finished! Completely finished!

The price He paid on the cross was enough to cover all my sin, and I finally allowed myself to experience the freedom that I had owned for so long. When I came to this realization, I was wandering all alone in the middle of the German forest. During my walk, I fell to my knees right there and wept in gratitude. I finally understood the magnitude of God's grace toward me. I understood how much it covered and how completely free a gift I had been given. No need for my effort to *be* good enough to please Him.

So when people ask me how I came to know the Lord, I tell them I was saved at age seven, but didn't fully understand grace until I was nineteen. I have heard from many people that they had a similar experience, where truth unfolded in waves over long periods of time.

The second half of my summer experience in Germany took the form of an outreach team in Düsseldorf with Operation Mobilization. I was a whole new person after accepting grace and allowing my past to be *finished* once and for all. But, the headaches persisted. By that time my guitarist friend had become more than just a mentor to me. He had become a romantic interest. I was attracted to his deep walk with God as much as anything else. He came to visit me in Düsseldorf and took me out to dinner. As we walked along the Rhine River at sunset with birds fluttering above our heads (what an idyllic scene) I began to feel that familiar pounding in my head. I was getting another migraine.

I told my friend that he would need to drop me back off at the women's dormitory, where the ladies on my team were staying, so I could take a tranquilizer and knock myself out before it got too much worse. I will never forget what happened next.

He asked me a simple question, "Courtney, how big is your God?" I replied, "Well, He's very big . . . but I'm getting a migraine and need to take a pill to knock myself out for eight hours."

Since I hadn't gotten his point the first time, he repeated the question, "How big is your God?" Then it hit me all at once, the point that he was trying to get across. My God was so big that He could forgive me once and for all, for my sins. He was so big that He could heal me of my headaches. I did not need to suffer with migraines anymore and I really believed the Lord could heal me. I believed He was big enough to work miracles on my behalf.

So we bowed our heads and prayed for that healing. The headache just went away. That had never happened before, every time a migraine headache began, it just took over. Never had one just disappeared. I knew something amazing had just happened. I knew I was free from sin and now I was also free from the incapacitating migraines, which I had suffered from for years.

I took the prescription bottles out of my purse and threw them into the Rhine River. That was an act of faith, because I still had three weeks left in Germany, and I knew that if I had another headache, they would probably have to rush me to an emergency room for relief.

I have never had another migraine! It has been over 20 years now, and I no longer have migraines. Has God ever worked a miracle for you? Have you ever seen His signs and wonders first hand?

Maybe the weight of your sin has led to migraines, or stomach ulcers, or even heart attacks. Your body was never intended to carry around that much stress and burden. Maybe it is time for you to believe Jesus when He said, "It is finished."

Since that time, I have seen God do amazing things for me and for those around me. After relaying this testimony, I have prayed with at least two other women for the healing of their migraines. They, too, have been healed. So, do I believe in the power of prayer? Indeed I do! Do I believe that God not only exists, but is powerful enough to work miracles in our presence? Indeed I do!

THOUGHT QUESTIONS FOR CHAPTER 4

1. How lost were you before you were found? Take a minute to remember.
2. What is your story of salvation? How did God reveal Himself to you? When is the last time you told somebody that story?
3. Why is it so difficult to accept a gift without working for it? Who do you know that needs to hear your story of salvation?
4. How much has God's grace covered in your life?
5. Are there still things that you have held onto? Things that Jesus said were finished?
6. How big is *your* God?

SECTION II

Testing the Lord

5

Testing Is Not Always A Bad Thing

Most of us have been taught that asking God for miracles is a bad thing. Testing is typically seen in a negative light in the English language. If someone says you are *testy*, that usually means that you are in a bad mood. When you are *testing*, you are pushing or taunting someone with the intent to frustrate them. We take testing to mean challenging the authority of God. Somehow in colloquial English the definition of testing has taken on an entirely negative connotation.

On the other hand, you have heard the expression *testing the waters*. It refers to seeing how fast the current is moving before stepping in and being completely swept away by it. In this respect, testing is a good thing. To test is not always negative according to the context of Scripture either. There are examples where testing is not only allowed it is commanded. In fact, in 1 John 4:1–3, the Apostle teaches us to *test the spirits* to see what is true:

> [1]Beloved, do not believe every spirit, but test the spirits to see whether they are from God, because many false prophets have gone out into the world.
> [2]By this you know the Spirit of God: every spirit that confesses that Jesus Christ has come in the flesh is from God;
> [3]and every spirit that does not confess Jesus is not from God; this is the *spirit* of the antichrist, of which you have heard that it is coming, and now it is already in the world.

Another noteworthy example of a Biblical term which can take on a positive, as well as negative, meaning in the Bible is *leaven*. There are many times we find the use of an analogy of leaven (or yeast). Depending on the usage and the context, leaven can be an example of a good thing or a bad thing as it permeates the entire lump of dough. Good yeast yields a good lump of dough, while bad yeast yields a bad lump of dough.

In Matthew 16:6–12, the disciples are confused by Jesus cautioning them:

> [6]And Jesus said to them, "Watch out and beware of the leaven of the Pharisees and Sadducees."
> [7]They began to discuss this among themselves, saying, "He said that because we did not bring any bread."
> [8]But Jesus, aware of this, said, "You men of little faith, why do you discuss among yourselves that you have no bread?
> [9]Do you not yet understand or remember the five loaves of the five thousand, and how many baskets full you picked up?
> [10]Or the seven loaves of the four thousand, and how many large baskets full you picked up?
> [11]How is it that you do not understand that I did not speak to you concerning bread? But beware of the leaven of the Pharisees and Sadducees."
> [12]Then they understood that He did not say to beware of the leaven of bread, but of the teaching of the Pharisees and Sadducees.

At first they thought He was speaking about literal bread, but later understood that He meant that the teaching of these two groups was dangerous because it could spread as quickly as leaven through dough. Leaven continues to take on a negative connotation in I Corinthians 5:6–13:

> [6]Your boasting is not good. Do you not know that a little leaven leavens the whole lump of dough?
> [7]Clean out the old leaven so that you may be a new lump, just as you are in fact unleavened. For Christ our Passover also has been sacrificed.
> [8]Therefore let us celebrate the feast, not with old leaven, nor with the leaven of malice and wickedness, but with the unleavened bread of sincerity and truth.
> [9]I wrote you in my letter not to associate with immoral people;
> [10]I did not at all mean with the immoral people of this world, or with the covetous and swindlers, or with idolaters, for then you would have to go out of the world.
> [11]But actually, I wrote to you not to associate with any *so-called brother* if he is an immoral person, or covetous, or an idolater, or a reviler, or a drunkard, or a swindler—not even to eat with such a one.

> [12]For what have I to do with judging outsiders? Do you not judge those who are within the church?
> [13]But those who are outside, God judges. Remove the wicked man from among yourselves.

Paul encourages the Corinthian church to clean house and remove *so-called brothers* from among the church. Their presence, if allowed to remain within the church, could contaminate it, just like yeast moves quickly through dough.

If you have ever witnessed bread being baked, you get a clear picture of just how quickly yeast can double and triple the dough once you have added the activated yeast. If you haven't, it makes a fun science experiment. When mixed with warm water, granules of dry yeast spring into action and are ready to multiply and spread throughout the entire lump of dough in a matter of minutes. The recipe often calls for allowing the dough to sit and *rise* and then actually beating it back down with your fists before allowing the dough to rise once more.

It was a vivid warning to the church about how quickly the wrong teaching can spread throughout the church and one they would have easily understood. You can beat it down, but it will just keep on spreading. Paul tells them to remove immoral persons from their midst, before the leavening process swallows up the church in immorality.

But, we also find one positive use of the term leaven in Scripture as well. In both Matthew 13:33 as well as its companion reference Luke 13:21, we find the parable of leaven told by Jesus. Matthew 13:33 states:

> [33]He spoke another parable to them, "The kingdom of heaven is like leaven, which a woman took and hid in three pecks of flour until it was all leavened."

And, Luke 13:21 reiterates the same:

> [21]"It is like leaven, which a woman took and hid in three pecks of flour until it was all leavened."

In comparing the kingdom of heaven (obviously a positive comparison) he said it was like leaven. Just like the parable of the mustard seed which precedes it in both cases, leaven is an example of a small granule which grows into something large. In this instance leaven is seen as a *good* thing which grows into a *great* thing, ultimately the Kingdom of God.

The idea is that yeast permeates the entire lump of dough, it affects whatever it touches. So, if your leaven is bad, such as boasting or the false teaching of the Pharisees and Sadducees, it will affect all who come in contact with it. In this sense it is like a virus that spreads within a community. But if the leaven is good, such as the Kingdom of God, then the Gospel can spread just as rapidly as yeast can infiltrate an entire lump of dough.

So, the use of yeast, as an illustration in Scripture, can take both a positive as well as negative connotation. The idea of *testing* is used in Scripture in much the same way, both in positive as well as negative contexts. But, for some reason we only hear of it in a negative light. So, based on that faulty reasoning, the universal prohibition on testing God by praying for miracles is derived.

We have been taught that testing in the Bible is always negative. In this chapter I will show you that *testing* can also be good and even something God has called us to do. Just like the case of leaven, testing can take on both a positive and a negative meaning in Scripture. It all depends on the context.

Our deeply rooted belief that testing is always negative comes in large measure from the misinterpreted passage where Christ quotes Deuteronomy to Satan during His temptation in the wilderness. For some reason, this passage is almost universally understood to mean that requesting miracles and signs is the same thing as *testing the Lord your God*. So much so, that even well-trained Bible scholars take this section out of context, and preach entire sermons on the sinfulness of praying for miracles, using the temptations of Christ as their singular springboard.

Many of you have, no doubt, heard a sermon about this subject, and all that you came away with was the phrase, "Thou shall not test the Lord your God." You have been told that it is a stern warning to never be so bold as to ask God to perform a miracle, because obviously *thou shall not test Him*. That is not accurate and it takes the quote completely out of its original context. Let's explore that passage. I think you will find that it has been misinterpreted and misapplied more times than not.

The primary passage in question is that of the temptation of Christ found in Matthew 4:1–11. We all know the story, so read along with me as we explore the text again:

Testing Is Not Always A Bad Thing

*¹*Then Jesus was led up by the Spirit into the wilderness to be tempted by the devil.
*²*And after He had fasted forty days and forty nights, He then became hungry.
*³*And the tempter came and said to Him, "If You are the Son of God, command that these stones become bread."
*⁴*But He answered and said, "It is written, 'Man shall not live on bread alone, but on every word that proceeds out of the mouth of God.'"
*⁵*Then the devil took Him into the holy city and had Him stand on the pinnacle of the temple,
*⁶*and said to Him, "If You are the Son of God, throw Yourself down; for it is written, 'He will command His angels concerning you; and on their hands they will bear you up, so that you will not strike your foot against a stone.'"
*⁷*Jesus said to him, "On the other hand, it is written, 'You shall not put the Lord your God to the test.'"
*⁸*Again, the devil took Him to a very high mountain and showed Him all the kingdoms of the world and their glory;
*⁹*and he said to Him, "All these things I will give You, if You fall down and worship me."
*¹⁰*Then Jesus said to him, "Go, Satan! For it is written, 'You shall worship the Lord your God, and serve Him only.'"
*¹¹*Then the devil left Him; and behold, angels came and began to minister to Him.

Every time Satan tempts Christ, he is not just tempting the Lord to fulfill the desires of His flesh, (food, security, or fame) he is tempting Christ to totally undermine God's plan for salvation. If Christ had given in on any of these three temptations, He would have revealed His glory too soon and utterly destroyed our hope of salvation—His perfect sacrifice on the cross and resurrection three days later, His payment in full for the debt that we owed.

In each of his temptations, Satan asked Jesus to perform a miracle. But of course, Satan was *not* asking with pure motives, he was asking in an attempt to trip Christ up on each point. So, to determine that our asking for miracles is the same as Satan asking for miracles, is erroneous. They are not equivalent, since our motivation is not to trip Him up or prove Him false. To teach that since it was obviously evil on Satan's part, it is evil on our part, is illogical.

Praying for Miracles

That is the first issue I'd like to refute. You cannot equate Satan's evil and impure request for miracles with that of true believers with pure motives. Just because it was obviously evil coming from Satan, it does not equate that requesting God to be God and perform miracles is necessarily evil on behalf of Christians. You simply cannot interject that conclusion.

Then, there is the much maligned verse 7, which states:

> ⁷Jesus said to him, "On the other hand, it is written, 'You shall not put the Lord your God to the test.'"

Each time Satan makes his request for a miracle, he quotes Scripture out of context to the Lord. Each time Christ quotes Scripture right back, but in its proper context, to refute the Devil's lies. The context is the key! It is interesting that Jesus chooses His quotes all three times directly from the book of Deuteronomy. That is the context which the quote, "You shall not put the Lord your God to the test," comes from.

To understand the meaning of the quote, we must first go back to the original passage in Deuteronomy 6 and study through verses 13–16. Then the reason for Christ's quote comes to light. In Deuteronomy 6:13–16, God is commanding the Israelites about what true worship looks like. It says:

> ¹³"You shall fear only the Lord your God; and you shall worship Him and swear by His name.
> ¹⁴You shall not follow other gods, any of the gods of the peoples who surround you,
> ¹⁵for the Lord your God in the midst of you is a jealous God; otherwise the anger of the Lord your God will be kindled against you, and He will wipe you off the face of the earth.
> ¹⁶You shall not put the Lord your God to the test, as you tested Him at Massah."

Well, that changes everything. Do you remember what almost happened to the Israelites back at Massah? That was the first time God threatened to wipe out the whole nation of Israel due to their disobedience. That is the context of the quote. God tells Moses in Exodus 32:10:

> ¹⁰Now then let Me alone, that My anger may burn against them and that I may destroy them; and I will make of you a great nation.

Just like He cleaned house with the worldwide flood and started over again with Noah and his family, God was thinking about cleaning house of the entire nation of Israel and starting over with Moses and his family. Moses intervened, as the nation's mediator, and begged God to spare them. The result being found in Exodus 32:14:

> *14*So the Lord changed His mind about the harm which He said He would do to His people.

So, in this section of Deuteronomy 6, God is reminding His nation, how close they came to destruction. He says not to test Him like that again. The word *test* here has nothing whatsoever to do with asking for a miracle. Its meaning is more that of tempting His anger. God is saying don't tempt me people, I could decide to wipe you off the face of the earth. In essence, don't push me to that kind of anger again. Don't try my patience. That doesn't sound anything like the way you have probably heard it preached, does it? But, in context, that is what *test* means here.

So, Jesus quotes only that portion to Satan. In this context, it was meant as a direct threat! Satan knows full-well that his ultimate doom and destruction are in the forecast. He is very aware of his future destiny, being thrown into the lake of fire. Revelation 20:10 states:

> *10*And the devil who deceived them was thrown into the lake of fire and brimstone, where the beast and the false prophet are also; and they will be tormented day and night forever and ever.

Satan knows that his dominion on earth will ultimately come to an end, and so will he. He knows how this story ends, and what his fate will be.

Basically, Jesus is warning Satan that He could choose to wipe him off the face of the earth any time He wants to, so don't push Him. It has nothing at all to do with the fact that Satan requested for Jesus to perform a miracle. It was meant as a strong rebuke and stern warning to the Devil.

The account of this same temptation of Christ by Satan, in the Gospel of Luke, also takes place in chapter 4, but in this version the events are in a different order. In Luke 4:12 we find the famous quote:

> *12*And Jesus answered and said to him, "It is said, 'You shall not put the Lord your God to the test.'"

We see from the very next verse in Luke 4:13 that Satan understood the warning and departed immediately after that:

> *13*When the devil had finished every temptation, he left Him until an opportune time.

Satan was out of there in a flash when he heard Christ's quote. He heard Christ's threat and decided to exit stage left. Satan understood the context of the quote and heard its implication loud and clear.

Taken out of context and relying only upon our colloquial English understanding of the word *test*, I can see how it has been interpreted that we should never test the Lord by asking for miracles, like Satan did. But, that is absolutely not the point here. When we study the quote in context it makes perfect sense. "Don't test the Lord your God," was a specific warning and a direct threat to Satan, not to anger God enough to destroy him right then and right there. The quote was in essence saying, Satan you know your fate, don't push me. It was never meant as a general prohibition for all believers to not test the Lord by requesting Him to perform a miracle. That is an assumption that has often been made and it makes no sense to take that giant leap of both interpretation and application.

Psalm 95 gives even more insight into this passage. Check out verses 7–11:

> [7]"For He is our God, and we are the people of His pasture and the sheep of His hand, today if you would hear His voice,
> [8]Do not harden your hearts, as at Meribah, as in the day of Massah in the wilderness,
> [9]When your fathers tested Me, they tried Me, though they had seen My work.
> [10]For forty years I loathed that generation, and said they are a people who err in their heart, and they do not know My ways.
> [11]Therefore I swore in My anger, truly they shall not enter into My rest."

If you remember the story, thanks in part to Moses' intervention and mediation on behalf of the nation, God relented. He decided not to wipe the entire nation off the face of the Earth. Instead, He told them that their unbelieving generation would not step foot in the Promised Land. So, they wandered in the dessert for forty years as that generation slowly died off.

That was God's punishment on that unbelieving generation, they did not get to step foot in the Promised Land. After forty years the only elders left where Joshua, Caleb and Moses. Joshua and Caleb, as you recall, were the only two original spies who went to spy out the land and believed God would deliver it into the hands of Israel as He had promised. They were the only spies who came back with a good report. So, they were the only ones of that generation who were allowed to live and to enter into the Promised Land.

Numbers 14:36–38 tells the story:

> [36]As for the men whom Moses sent to spy out the land and who returned and made all the congregation grumble against Him by bringing out a bad report concerning the land,
> [37]even those men who brought out the very bad report of the land died by a plague before the Lord.
> [38]But Joshua the son of Nun and Caleb the son of Jephunneh remained alive out of those men who went to spy out the land.

So, as we have seen, our general understanding of the famous quote "Do not put the Lord your God to the test," is actually based upon a misunderstanding of a familiar passage taken completely out of context. God does not consider it *testing* Him in a negative sense, if we ask Him to be true to His majestic nature and perform miracles, signs and wonders that only He can do. The Biblical account of Christ's temptation by Satan is not intended to prohibit all believers from *testing* the Lord by asking for Him to perform miracles, although that is what many of us have been taught all our lives.

So, the next time you hear about testing the Lord, make sure to explore the context surrounding it. Asking for God to be God and perform miracles in not prohibited based on these passages. In fact there are times when it is prescribed by God Himself. He is ready to amaze His people if only they will ask as Psalm 34:8 encourages:

> [8] O taste and see that the LORD is good;
> How blessed is the man who takes refuge in Him!

THOUGHT QUESTIONS FOR CHAPTER 5

1. What was your original understanding of the passage we just explored regarding Christ's temptation by Satan?
2. After studying the context, what new understanding has emerged?
3. How would you define the way Satan tested the Lord?
4. Does that prohibit you from requesting God to perform a miracle?
5. Have you ever tested God in a negative way? In a positive way?
6. What does the phrase "Do not put the Lord your God to the test," mean to you now?

6

Isn't Praying for Miracles A Sin?

ALONG WITH THE MISCONCEPTION that *testing the Lord* is always negative, many of us have also been taught that praying for miracles and asking God to perform signs is an equally bad thing to do. In fact, according to some, asking for miracles is a sin. But, Jesus actually commended those who sought His miracles in faith. He only rebuked those who sought a sign with improper motives. Some, like the Pharisees and Sadducees, wanted nothing more than to find fault with Jesus. When they sought a miracle it was for no other reason than to prove Him false. While others sought miracles without faith.

Apart from faith, and with impure motives, seeking a sign *is* sin. But, that does not mean that those who ask with faith and with pure motives are also sinful if they ask God to perform miracles, signs and wonders.

In fact, God never rebukes or condemns these kinds of faithful believers when they ask for miraculous things. He does not just provide a sign begrudgingly, as if to throw a bone to weak believer who is just craving a sign. He does so with vigor and delight as He engages in a two-way conversation with a beloved child.

I have always envisioned God as sitting on the edge of His throne just waiting for His children to trust in Him enough to ask big things of Him. Matthew 7:7–11 agrees. In this passage Christ commands that we be obedient followers and ask God to be God:

> [7]"Ask, and it will be given to you; seek, and you will find; knock, and it will be opened to you.

> ⁸For everyone who asks receives, and he who seeks finds, and to him who knocks it will be opened.
> ⁹Or what man is there among you who, when his son asks for a loaf, will give him a stone?
> ¹⁰Or if he asks for a fish, he will not give him a snake, will he?
> ¹¹If you then, being evil, know how to give good gifts to your children, how much more will your Father who is in heaven give what is good to those who ask Him!"

God wants us to ask Him for good gifts. He wants us to be amazed by His works and His provision. But, God is not an overbearing or meddlesome Father. He doesn't interfere, rather He waits patiently for His children to ask Him. It is okay for us to ask big things, to seek His signs and wonders, and to be persistent in our request. Just like a father, God wants to give us good gifts. We are taught to ask, seek and to continue knocking at His door until we receive. Again, there is no rebuke found in this teaching, rather Christ commands us to ask, seek and knock.

When we get to Heaven, once we have finished asking all those questions that we have been stock-piling throughout our lives, I'll bet God's main question for us will be why we didn't ask Him for more. He was ready, willing and able to meet all our needs. He was just waiting to be asked.

The faith it takes to ask God to do something completely out the ordinary, something undeniably divine, is something that brings joy to our Father. He actually longs to be tested and found worthy and amazing. He loves our praise and He also loves our trust. God honors the great faith it takes for His servants to request Him to perform miracles. So, you see, testing can also be a good thing, the difference is in the heart.

Here is a surprise. God actually commands us to test Him in some passages, like Malachi 3:10. In this passage we are encouraged to test Him and see that He is who He claims to be. That is very different from testing Him to prove Him false or unreliable. God welcomes one form of testing, while He despises the other.

Let's look at both forms of testing, found back to back in one brief passage. Malachi 3:7–15, has an example of both positive and negative testing:

> ⁷"From the days of your fathers you have turned aside from My statutes and have not kept them. Return to Me, and I will return to you," says the Lord of hosts. "But you say, 'How shall we return?'

Isn't Praying for Miracles A Sin?

> ⁸Will a man rob God? Yet you are robbing Me! But you say, 'How have we robbed You?' In tithes and offerings.
> ⁹You are cursed with a curse, for you are robbing Me, the whole nation of you!
> ¹⁰Bring the whole tithe into the storehouse, so that there may be food in My house, and *test* Me now in this," says the Lord of hosts, "if I will not open for you the windows of heaven and pour out for you a blessing until it overflows.
> ¹¹ Then I will rebuke the devourer for you, so that it will not destroy the fruits of the ground; nor will your vine in the field cast its grapes," says the Lord of hosts.
> ¹²"All the nations will call you blessed, for you shall be a delightful land," says the Lord of hosts.
> ¹³"Your words have been arrogant against Me," says the Lord. "Yet you say, 'What have we spoken against You?'
> ¹⁴You have said, 'It is vain to serve God; and what profit is it that we have kept His charge, and that we have walked in mourning before the Lord of hosts?
> ¹⁵So now we call the arrogant blessed; not only are the doers of wickedness built up but they also *test* God and escape.'"

God actually commanded His faithful people to *test* Him and find Him to be good and true! Here is the example of testing shown in a positive light. In Malachi 3:10 we read:

> ¹⁰"Bring the whole tithe into the storehouse, so that there may be food in My house, and test Me now in this," says the Lord of hosts, "if I will not open for you the windows of heaven and pour out for you a blessing until it overflows."

In other words . . . just try Me. He promises that He is good for His word and He stands ready to prove Himself to anyone who questions His veracity. This passage proves that testing God is not universally prohibited, just like the opposite uses of the word leaven which we explored in the last chapter.

God is good. He is true to His word. He intends to bless those who trust in His name. And amazingly, He not only invites believers to try Him out, He challenges them to do so if they are not sure or lack faith. He actually throws down a challenge intended to bolster our faith. If we do what we are instructed to do, namely bring the whole tithe into the storehouse, He stands prepared to amaze us and build our faith by opening the windows of heaven and pouring out blessings until they overflow.

Wow! God says if we take Him up on this challenge, He guarantees the outcome of blessing. Anyone who has ever faithfully tried what God states in this verse knows what overflowing blessing looks like. Come on, give it a try. See that He is true to His word.

Then, we see the word test used in a negative way. God says that His people *test* Him, not believing that He will provide righteous judgment for sin. In Malachi 3:15 He says:

> [15]"'So now we call the arrogant blessed; not only are the doers of wickedness built up but they also test God and escape.'"

In this sense *test* means that the people are pushing God to act on His righteous judgment and punish the wicked. Just like the testing we saw earlier in Deuteronomy, they were literally egging Him on to wrath. It might look like a child using little stick to play with a bear trap which is set and ready to spring, just waiting to see if and when it will snap.

Isn't it funny that when we feel we have been mistreated, the one thing we want most of all is God's justice. But, when we have been the one doing the mistreating (in this case mistreating God Himself) the last thing we want or expect is God's justice.

The people were dismissing God's righteous anger and did not expect Him to punish their sin. This form of testing is definitely negative, but it is interesting to find both examples back to back in the same passage. Somehow people ignore the positive instances of testing and only focus on the negative ones.

Let's explore this idea of *testing* a little more. Another example of this issue is found again in Psalm 78. Here we find the history of Israel briefly described. The nation was commanded to recount all of God's miraculous works throughout their generations. Psalm 78:4 states:

> [4]We will not conceal them from their children, but tell to the generation to come the praises of the Lord, and His strength and His wondrous works that He has done.

The Psalm goes on to tell of how the unbelieving generation who perished in the desert just short of the Promised Land had gone astray in their heart. It lists God's miracles and signs which had been performed on their behalf, in order to build their faith and prepare them to inhabit the Land. It also reminds the nation of the many times they had tempted God to anger. In Psalm78:14–18, notice that verse 18 uses the word *test*:

> [14] Then He led them with the cloud by day
> And all the night with a light of fire.
> [15] He split the rocks in the wilderness
> And gave them abundant drink like the ocean depths.
> [16] He brought forth streams also from the rock
> And caused waters to run down like rivers.
> [17] Yet they still continued to sin against Him,
> To rebel against the Most High in the desert.
> [18] And in their heart they put God to the test
> By asking food according to their desire.

Moving on . . . verses 41 and 56 use the word *tempted*, while verse 58 says they *provoked* Him, but all have the same connotation:

> [56] Yet they *tempted* and rebelled against the Most High God
> And did not keep His testimonies,
> [57] But turned back and acted treacherously like their fathers;
> They turned aside like a treacherous bow.
> [58] For they *provoked* Him with their high places
> And aroused His jealousy with their graven images.

This Psalm reminds the nation of Israel about all the fabulous miracles God had performed in their sight. It recalls many of the amazing miracles, wonders, and works God had showed to His people beginning with securing their freedom from Egypt. It tells of how He led them and fed them during the dessert wanderings.

Throughout Psalm 78, we see the unfaithful heart of the people contrasted with the righteous integrity of God's heart. Nowhere in this Psalm were the Israelites condemned for praying for God to perform miracles, only for their subsequent lack of faith in God, and for forgetting the wonders He had performed in their sight. The miracles were intended to build the faith of the people, but God's wondrous signs would not keep them from rebelling and acting treacherously toward Him.

Time and again the writer reminds Israel how faithless they were and how they refused to trust in God with their whole heart. Verses 40–43 states:

> [40] How often they rebelled against Him in the wilderness
> And grieved Him in the desert!
> [41] Again and again they *tempted* God,
> And pained the Holy One of Israel.
> [42] They did not remember His power,

Praying for Miracles

> The day when He redeemed them from the adversary,
> ⁴³When He performed His signs in Egypt
> And His marvels in the field of Zoan.

God provided proof and gave them ample reason to believe and trust in Him, but they refused and *tested* his patience over and over, until finally God allowed for another time of distress, when the Ark of the Covenant was captured by the Philistines. Perhaps difficulties would get their attention, since His miracles had somehow failed to do the trick.

In this Psalm we see that God makes provisions for the weak faith of men. He reveals Himself and continues to work miracles to bolster their confidence and solidify their faith. That was His plan and desire for His people, the Israelites. It was a lesson that Israel had to learn and relearn. It is a lesson we often have to learn and relearn as well. Just like the Israelites who had witnessed God's miraculous power, we too, have seen His power but are just not sure He is really capable of doing those things for us, or of doing them for us one more time. So often we allow our circumstance to seem bigger than our God. So in our littleness of faith, we fail to ask God to perform miracles. We forget who our Father is and what He is capable of doing on our behalf.

St. Augustine pondered why God chose to perform miracles in our sight. When reflecting upon the miracles recorded in the New Testament, those performed by Christ, he stated this:

> The miracles wrought by our Lord Jesus Christ are truly divine works, and they are a lesson to the human mind to see God in visible things. But because God is not visible to mortal eyes, and His miracles, by which He governs the whole world and all creatures, have ceased to cause wonder by reason of their frequency, so that hardly anyone will deign to consider the great and stupendous works of God in each separate seed; according to that mercy of His He reserved to Himself certain things which He would do in their appointed time above the usual and ordinary course of nature, that men, who made light of everyday miracles, seeing not greater, but unusual ones, might wonder and be amazed. For the government of the whole universe is a greater miracle than feeding five thousand men on loaves. Still no man wonders at the first, whereas men wonder at the second, not because it is greater, but because it is rarer.[1]

---

1. Allies, *Leaves from St. Augustine*, 227.

On the other hand, there comes a time when God has provided all the reassurance and proof that men need and He chooses to stop providing more evidence. I am not saying God uses miracles to maintain our faith, just that He uses them to grow our faith. If He stopped performing signs and wonders, our memory of His past wonders should be enough to sustain us. The point is that the nation should have been able to recall all those miracles for themselves. If the heart doesn't change and if the faith doesn't grow after witnessing God's amazing power time and again, then there comes a time when no further signs will be offered. This principle is seen vividly in the story of the rich man and Lazarus in Luke 16:19–31:

> [19]"Now there was a rich man, and he habitually dressed in purple and fine linen, joyously living in splendor every day.
>
> [20]And a poor man named Lazarus was laid at his gate, covered with sores,
>
> [21]and longing to be fed with the crumbs which were falling from the rich man's table; besides, even the dogs were coming and licking his sores.
>
> [22]Now the poor man died and was carried away by the angels to Abraham's bosom; and the rich man also died and was buried.
>
> [23]In Hades he lifted up his eyes, being in torment, and saw Abraham far away and Lazarus in his bosom.
>
> [24]And he cried out and said, 'Father Abraham, have mercy on me, and send Lazarus so that he may dip the tip of his finger in water and cool off my tongue, for I am in agony in this flame.'
>
> [25]But Abraham said, 'Child, remember that during your life you received your good things, and likewise Lazarus bad things; but now he is being comforted here, and you are in agony.
>
> [26]And besides all this, between us and you there is a great chasm fixed, so that those who wish to come over from here to you will not be able, and that none may cross over from there to us.'
>
> [27]And he said, 'Then I beg you, father, that you send him to my father's house—
>
> [28]for I have five brothers—in order that he may warn them, so that they will not also come to this place of torment.'
>
> [29]But Abraham said, 'They have Moses and the Prophets; let them hear them.'
>
> [30]But he said, 'No, father Abraham, but if someone goes to them from the dead, they will repent!'
>
> [31]But he said to him, 'If they do not listen to Moses and the Prophets, they will not be persuaded even if someone rises from the dead.'"

God provided ample proof to the nation of Israel, the same way the rich man's brothers had been taught by Moses and the Prophets all they needed to know in order to have faith in God. The rich man is not given a name in this story. But the poor man is given a name, the same name as that of Jesus' close friend Lazarus, who was literally raised by Jesus from the dead. Christ had performed that awesome miracle already, prior to this parable being told.

I think this story is so poignant because Jesus was foretelling the fact that even when He would die by crucifixion and be raised again from the dead on the third day, even that would not provide enough proof for so many in Israel to believe.

Not even a miracle like bodily resurrection might be enough to convince some people. So, don't exhaust God by continually seeking a sign in order to believe. That is not what I am advocating in this book. As Christians we should not always be starting over from square one, we should grow, and our experiences as well as our growing relationship with the Lord, should be enough proof for us.

I am not saying that we should need constant reassurance of the truth that is within us, only that God still chooses to grow our faith by displaying His miraculous power. Praying for God to perform miracles is not equivalent to *testing* Him in a negative sense, and it is not a sin. God desires for us to ask Him for big things and loves to come through in miraculous ways. It is one legitimate way that He chooses to build our faith. Jesus spent a lot of time teaching about prayer, and He always advocated asking God for big things.

THOUGHT QUESTIONS FOR CHAPTER 6

1. What have you been taught about asking God for miracles?
2. What does Christ's teaching about asking, seeking and knocking mean to you? Have you ever done it? What was the result?
3. What do you think about God's command to test him in Malachi? Had you ever noticed that passage before?
4. Why does the Psalmist spend so much time recounting to Israel, the miracles they had witnessed?
5. When is the last time you recounted all that you have witnessed God do in your life? Isn't that the point of keeping a prayer journal?
6. How does the story of the Rich Man and Lazarus impact you?

7

Doesn't It Mean I Am An Immature Believer?

WE HAVE ALL HEARD numerous sermons about the pitfalls of testing and how those who test the Lord are lacking faith and are simply immature Christians. Multitudes have been led to believe that those spiritual pigmy's who lack the faith to *just believe* were placed on the pages of Scripture as a warning to the rest of us.

Abraham, Gideon, Jonah, Peter and Thomas have familiar stories that we would never dare repeat with the benefit of our hind-sight vision. But don't be so hard on these guys. Would you have done anything differently? They are human just like us. They failed to believe in God's power at times, but God chose to work with them and carry them through to the finish line. I am so thankful that some of the biggest failures in the Bible went on to become patriarchs, prophets and apostles. That is encouraging news for all of us.

Requesting proof is not the hallmark of immaturity, although it has gotten a bad rap, and I think incorrectly so. As we saw in the last chapter God provides us with signs as ample proof in order to build our faith. The more we see of His power, the easier it is to trust Him. He delights in revealing Himself to His children, so they can learn to trust Him more deeply and more completely.

God never calls us to *blind faith*, that is faith without a basis. He is the basis! Remember, Christ did not call Peter to step out of the boat and walk on water without first showing him that walking on water was possible. Christ gave Peter something, and more importantly *someone*, to put his faith in. We are so quick to criticize Peter for his doubt and lack of faith. Revisit the story with me in Matthew 14:25–33:

> [25] And in the fourth watch of the night He came to them, walking on the sea.
> [26] When the disciples saw Him walking on the sea, they were terrified, and said, "It is a ghost!" And they cried out in fear.
> [27] But immediately Jesus spoke to them, saying, "Take courage, it is I; do not be afraid."
> [28] Peter said to Him, "Lord, if it is You, command me to come to You on the water."
> [29] And He said, "Come!" And Peter got out of the boat, and walked on the water and came toward Jesus.
> [30] But seeing the wind, he became frightened, and beginning to sink, he cried out, "Lord, save me!"
> [31] Immediately Jesus stretched out His hand and took hold of him, and said to him, "You of little faith, why did you doubt?"
> [32] When they got into the boat, the wind stopped.
> [33] And those who were in the boat worshiped Him, saying, "You are certainly God's Son!"

A few things probably stand out to you when you read the entire passage in context. First, whose idea was it for Peter to step out of the boat and walk to Jesus on the water? That's right, Peter proposed it himself! Bet you never saw that little detail before. He thought it was possible and knew that with the help of the Lord it could be done. That is an important tidbit that is so often ignored. Jesus didn't command Peter to come to Him, as the story is so often misquoted. He encouraged Peter to walk to Him after Peter first suggested doing so. Peter saw that walking on water was possible, since Jesus was doing it, and had enough faith to believe that, with God's help, he could walk on water too.

Secondly, Peter actually stepped out of the boat, and began to do just that, walk on water! When we recall the story, all we usually envision is Peter thrashing about in the sea, needing to be rescued. And, Jesus is positioned as his lifeguard, with hand outstretched. We are so focused on the reprimand he received when his faith waned, and he began to sink, that we lose sight of the fact that Peter actually *did* walk on water.

So, aside from Jesus Himself, Peter is the only other person in Scripture who can make that claim. He had enough faith to step out of the boat and begin walking on top of the wind-swept sea. But, we are so busy piously shaking our finger at Peter for his *doubt,* that we overlook his incredible journey. We just tend to focus on his failure rather than his triumph. It may have only been a few steps, but they were more powerful imprints than Neil Armstrong left on the surface of the moon. Peter's faith allowed him to walk on water!

Don't lose sight of one other fact. None of the other disciples asked for the opportunity to put their faith into action and walk to Jesus on the waves. None of them even considered it possible. The rest of the bunch just stood there and mutely observed Peter's brave steps of faith. It was an act of incredible faith to believe it could be accomplished and then to actually take those steps. Imagine how much faith it must have taken to swing that first leg over the side of the rocking boat.

The only thing I could liken it to would be the few times I have been rappelling. When you get all your gear on and check your harnesses and clips twice, you are left to trust two things: that the equipment, and your belay partner located at the bottom of the cliff, will both do their job. I'm not a big fan of heights anyway, so that first step backwards over the face of the cliff is always a doozey. You are literally fighting against all your natural inclinations for self-preservation. That is just what the Apostle Peter must have felt as his stomach found its way up to his throat and his heart began to race in fear.

In his book, *I Call It Heresy*, A. W. Tozer explored the Apostle Peter in great detail. He recalls Peter as a bundle of contradictions, great in faith, but also first to leap without looking:

> That was Peter—more daring than any of the apostles and often with more faith—but he had more daring than he had faith! Have you met any of God's children like that?
>
> You remember that Peter was so daring that he rushed out of the boat and actually walked on water, and yet he had such little faith that it would not support his daring. So he sank, and then had to be helped by the Lord to keep him from drowning![1]

Just think about it, if Peter had held his focus and continued to believe, he could have completed the trip without sinking and needing to be rescued. Let's cut Peter a little slack. It was his faithful expectation that led to his faithful act.

I wonder if the amazing adventure Peter had that night on the stormy sea, even though it ended with a reprimand and a rescue, taught Peter

---

1. Tozer, *I Call It Heresy*, 17.

about steps of faith and how they each build upon one another and lead onward to greater faith. I wonder if he was thinking about that very night that he walked on the sea, when he penned these verses in 2 Peter 1:5–11:

> ⁵Now for this very reason also, applying all diligence, in your faith supply moral excellence, and in your moral excellence, knowledge,
> ⁶and in your knowledge, self-control, and in your self-control, perseverance, and in your perseverance, godliness,
> ⁷and in your godliness, brotherly kindness, and in your brotherly kindness, love.
> ⁸For if these qualities are yours and are increasing, they render you neither useless nor unfruitful in the true knowledge of our Lord Jesus Christ.
> ⁹For he who lacks these qualities is blind or short-sighted, having forgotten his purification from his former sins.
> ¹⁰Therefore, brethren, be all the more diligent to make certain about His calling and choosing you; for as long as you practice these things, you will never stumble;
> ¹¹for in this way the entrance into the eternal kingdom of our Lord and Savior Jesus Christ will be abundantly supplied to you.

I sometimes refer to this passage as the stair-steps of faith. It is clear that Peter saw the spiritual life as a series of successive steps, each one building upon the one that went before it. Each step is important, each one takes faith. As a Christian walks through life, Peter says they won't be sidelined or become useless or unfruitful, and he specifically notes that as long as we walk in obedience we will never *stumble*. It looks like his personal experience walking toward Jesus on the water had a few take-aways for him. I am so glad he shared his experience with us. Just like Peter, we don't have to be perfect to be powerful.

But, for some reason, most of the time preachers spend on Peter focuses on beating him up for his impulsive behavior. Don't forget that same impulsive behavior led Peter to become one of Christ's first followers, in Mark 1:14–18:

> ¹⁴Now after John had been taken into custody, Jesus came into Galilee, preaching the gospel of God
> ¹⁵and saying, "The time is fulfilled, and the kingdom of God is at hand; repent and believe in the gospel."
> ¹⁶As He was going along by the Sea of Galilee, He saw Simon and Andrew, the brother of Simon, casting a net in the sea; for they were fishermen.

> [17] And Jesus said to them, "Follow Me, and I will make you become fishers of men."
> [18] Immediately they left their nets and followed Him.

So it seems there is also a place for being completely impetuous, at least when it comes to following Christ. We all know the caricature of Peter as the impulsive and, at times, even hot-headed disciple. He is often corrected and rebuked by Jesus. But, it was just that boldness and tenacity that led the Lord to praise this same flawed man in Matthew 16:15–19:

> [15] He said to them, "But who do you say that I am?"
> [16] Simon Peter answered, "You are the Christ, the Son of the living God."
> [17] And Jesus said to him, "Blessed are you, Simon Barjona, because flesh and blood did not reveal this to you, but My Father who is in heaven."
> [18] "I also say to you that you are Peter, and upon this rock I will build My church; and the gates of Hades will not overpower it."
> [19] "I will give you the keys of the kingdom of heaven; and whatever you bind on earth shall have been bound in heaven, and whatever you loose on earth shall have been loosed in heaven."

A commendation like that is reserved for a disciple like Peter. Peter boldly proclaimed, "You are the Christ, the Son of the living God." He did not need a minute to mull it over or word it right, he just blurted out what he knew to be true. Peter went on to become one of the boldest witnesses of Christ. His leadership was crucial to the foundation of the church and the spread of the faith beyond Jerusalem. Even a flawed and impulsive disciple can become a faithful follower and powerful person in God's Kingdom. Better to have tried and failed than to have never tried at all. There is hope for all of us.

THOUGHT QUESTIONS FOR CHAPTER 7

1. Why did Peter believe he could walk on water?
2. What was your view of Peter the first time you studied or were taught about this story?
3. How has your view of Peter changed?
4. Who would you have been more like in this story, bold Peter or the other mute disciples just watching it all happen?
5. How did this experience of taking steps, impact Peter's Christian life, and his teaching about how each step we take leads to another?
6. Are you bold, or even hot-headed like Peter at times? How can God use that impetuous streak for His glory?

8

Faithful or Faithless?

Now let's explore another similar disciple you have heard about: Doubting Thomas. Poor guy! Few other Biblical characters have had such an unflattering adjective forever attached to their name. He is never referred to as the Apostle Thomas, although that is his true claim to fame, as one of the twelve disciples hand-picked by Jesus to be His witnesses. Whenever we hear about Thomas, it's because of his doubting. In fact, that is just about the only thing we have recorded specifically about Thomas, other than his nickname Didymus, which simply tells us he was a twin.

We don't think much of him. He has become a whipping-boy to us, someone we love to beat up on, someone so easy to dismiss. The only other actual quote from Thomas in all of Scripture is found in John 11:16, when he shows his leadership among the disciples and his commitment to Christ, even if that were to lead to death. John 11:11–16 sets the scene:

> [11]This He said, and after that He said to them, "Our friend Lazarus has fallen asleep; but I go, so that I may awaken him out of sleep."
> [12]The disciples then said to Him, "Lord, if he has fallen asleep, he will recover."
> [13]Now Jesus had spoken of his death, but they thought that He was speaking of literal sleep.
> [14]So Jesus then said to them plainly, "Lazarus is dead,
> [15]and I am glad for your sakes that I was not there, so that you may believe; but let us go to him."
> [16]Therefore Thomas, who is called Didymus, said to his fellow disciples, "Let us also go, so that we may die with Him."

Although Thomas did not fully understand the miracle that he and his friends were about to witness, namely the raising of Lazarus from the dead, he was excited that Jesus had said it would be an opportunity for them to believe. Thomas thought that if it was a good thing for Lazarus to have died, then he was ready to do the same, ready to go to his own death. If Jesus meant that death was good for Lazarus, then it would be good for him too. Doesn't sound like a man of little faith to me. His own life was less important to him than the *belief* that Christ spoke of. He craved that above all else, even his own life.

In his commentary on the Gospel of John, Martin Luther explained the scene this way:

> For in the apostles we see what a poor thing the human heart is. Among them all, it seems, Thomas was the most daring and courageous when he said, "Let us also go that we may die with him;" then he also recently had seen how Christ raised up Lazarus; and yet he imagines that it is at an end with Jesus.[1]

I think Thomas has become too easy of a target for teachers and preachers. What I am about to lay out challenges what has been preached for so long, that it has become orthodox thought. Let's take another look at the all too familiar story of hard-hearted, unbelieving Thomas. Let's put ourselves in his shoes and look at the story in context for a change. Perhaps some different conclusions can be drawn from his request for proof of the Lord's resurrection.

His story is typically picked up in John 20:24–25, where we read:

> [24]But Thomas, one of the twelve, called Didymus, was not with them when Jesus came.
> [25]So the other disciples were saying to him, "We have seen the Lord!" But he said to them, "Unless I see in His hands the imprint of the nails, and put my finger into the place of the nails, and put my hand into His side, I will not believe."

That section is usually all that is referenced before the sermon unloads on Thomas for his unbelief. If you only read that section, it's easy to make a case for a *Doubting Thomas*. Based solely on this limited information, it is easy to single him out as the black-sheep of the apostolic bunch. Unfortunately many preachers have taken that lone passage out of context and used it as their singular jumping off point for a clever sermon.

1. Mueller, *Luther's Explanatory Notes on the Gospels*, 400.

I mean, that sounds pretty harsh of Thomas, for him to ask to touch the actual wounds on Christ's resurrected body, and a bit grotesque if you ask me. What kind of hard-hearted guy are we dealing with here? Who would even think of such a thing? But, if we take these two verses in context, an entirely different picture emerges.

The idea of actually touching the wounds in Christ's hands and side were not originated by Thomas. Did you realize that? He did not just think that up on his own, out of the clear blue. Let's back *way* up. Go back to the beginning of John chapter 20.

On Easter, Mary Magdalene was the first to discover that Jesus' body was missing from the tomb, early in the morning. Two disciples came with her and witnessed this for themselves, Peter and John. John 20:1–10 recounts the story:

> [1]Now on the first day of the week Mary Magdalene came early to the tomb, while it was still dark, and saw the stone already taken away from the tomb.
>
> [2]So she ran and came to Simon Peter and to the other disciple whom Jesus loved, and said to them, "They have taken away the Lord out of the tomb, and we do not know where they have laid Him."
>
> [3]So Peter and the other disciple went forth, and they were going to the tomb.
>
> [4]The two were running together; and the other disciple ran ahead faster than Peter and came to the tomb first;
>
> [5]and stooping and looking in, he saw the linen wrappings lying there; but he did not go in.
>
> [6]And so Simon Peter also came, following him, and entered the tomb; and he saw the linen wrappings lying there,
>
> [7]and the face-cloth which had been on His head, not lying with the linen wrappings, but rolled up in a place by itself.
>
> [8]So the other disciple who had first come to the tomb then also entered, and he saw and believed.
>
> [9]For as yet they did not understand the Scripture, that He must rise again from the dead.
>
> [10]So the disciples went away again to their own homes.

After looking into the tomb and seeing the linen wrappings and the face cloth were the only things left, they decided to go back home. What? They saw the evidence of the empty tomb and just went back into hiding, for fear of the Jewish leaders? Don't skip too quickly past this piece of the puzzle. No high-fives were exchanged, no fist-pumps, no preaching in the streets, no jumping for joy, no printing commemorative T-shirts emblazoned with the slogan *He Is Risen*. It just states plainly in verse 10:

> ¹⁰So the disciples went away again to their own homes.

So, why don't we label them Doubting Peter or Doubting John? They were presented with what they acknowledged to be compelling evidence of the resurrection of Jesus and it didn't change their lives or circumstances at all at this point in the story. They were in hiding, they went to inspect the empty tomb, and they went back into hiding. Wow!

After these two disciples leave, Mary is all alone weeping by the empty tomb, thinking that Jesus' body had either been stolen or moved. Jesus actually appears to her first. Now check out Mary's response to seeing the risen Christ. In verse 18 it says:

> ¹⁸Mary Magdalene came, announcing to the disciples, "I have seen the Lord," and that He had said these things to her.

Now you would expect the disciples would say something like, "Wow Mary, that's remarkable, tell us all about it!" But instead, they probably asked Mary to lock the door behind her and keep her voice down. That's right, the entire group of them, minus Thomas we later learn, just stayed locked up and huddled together the entire day in fear. Mary's astounding announcement didn't change their lives or their actions one little bit. So, why don't we label the whole bunch of them, (minus Thomas since he wasn't there to hear the joyful news), the doubting disciples?

John 20:19, goes on to explain:

> ¹⁹So when it was evening on that day, the first day of the week, and when the doors were shut where the disciples were, for fear of the Jews, Jesus came and stood in their midst and said to them, "Peace be with you."

Then Jesus offered the disciples the proof that He knew they would need in order to believe without ever being asked for it. Verse 20 continues:

> ²⁰And when He had said this, He showed them both His hands and His side. The disciples *then* rejoiced when they saw the Lord.

They *then* rejoiced. Only after Jesus showed them His hands and his side as proof, did they rejoice. Notice that the offer of physical proof was Jesus' idea, not any of the disciples, and it was certainly not Thomas' idea.

He wasn't even there! None of them thought to ask to see His hands or His side. That was the proof Jesus chose to offer to them without ever being asked for it.

Remember Thomas was absent when Jesus presented Himself and His hands and side as proof. So, perhaps in relaying the entire scene later to their good friend Thomas, after he rejoined them, they happened to mention exactly what they had seen, that Jesus had showed them His hands and His side as proof of His resurrection from the dead. Maybe that is where Thomas got the wild idea to ask for the exact same proof for himself that Jesus had already provided to the other ten disciples. The other ten, after all, had not been reprimanded for their unbelief. Jesus just knew they would need the evidence and so He provided it to them right off the bat. Christ knew they needed to see His hands and His side so they could *then* rejoice.

Now don't skip over the response of these disciples after seeing Jesus and being given adequate physical proof directly from the risen Lord. They went back into hiding! These bold heroes of the faith did what? John 20:26 tells us:

> [26] After eight days His disciples were again inside, and Thomas with them. Jesus came, the doors having been shut, and stood in their midst and said, "Peace be with you."

These spiritual giants, whose faith was supposedly so far superior to that of Thomas had locked themselves back up in a room together for fear of being arrested and crucified like Jesus had been. But, for some reason, we only single out Thomas as the *doubting* one. The other ten disciples had visually seen Jesus and even had opportunity to inspect His hands and side, and had been mulling over those awesome details for eight days! They not only had the word of Mary, but had visually seen Jesus' resurrected body with their own eyes.

To me this begs the question–do you think Thomas had as much trouble believing the messengers as he did the message? His fellow disciples tell him this life changing story about Jesus appearing to them in resurrected form, and they go right back into hiding. Hey, Thomas knew these guys really well. He had traveled with them, lived among them, and walked beside them for the past three years. He had seen their lack of faith, and mistakes that entire time. These guys were no spiritual giants

Faithful or Faithless?

and he knew it. Now they claim to have seen the Lord, and do nothing but continue hiding. Wouldn't you have questioned the messengers?

Going forward in this passage we see that in His second appearance to the disciples, Christ's first order of business was to offer the same proof to Thomas that he had previously offered the other ten disciples. Jesus didn't reprimand Thomas and say, "From this day forward your name shall be called, Doubting Thomas, because you are a big-fat-doubter." No, He said here is the same proof that I offered to the others, now believe. John 20:27–29 concludes the story:

> ²⁷Then He said to Thomas, "Reach here with your finger, and see My hands; and reach here your hand and put it into My side; and do not be unbelieving, but believing."
> ²⁸Thomas answered and said to Him, "My Lord and my God!"
> ²⁹Jesus said to him, "Because you have seen Me, have you believed? Blessed are they who did not see, and yet believed."

Notice also, that the text never tells us that any of the disciples, including Thomas, actually took the Lord up on His offer to touch His wounds. Although you may even recall seeing paintings of Thomas reaching out to touch the nail-scarred hands of Christ, reinforcing the image, that is not what the Bible says actually happened. The text does not say he reached out his hand to touch the Lord to finally satisfy his insatiable curiosity, only that Christ offered him the opportunity. In verse 28 we find Thomas' eloquent and sincere response to the proof he had witnessed, "Thomas answered and said to Him, 'My Lord and my God!'"

Don't minimize that response. No further investigation was needed. Thomas does not deserve the title *Doubting* Thomas ever again after that declaration of his belief in Christ's deity. If you want to label him as a doubter, then you can only legitimately pin that label on him for eight days out of his entire life. We have absolutely no evidence that Thomas had any doubting issues after his encounter with the risen Lord. He doubted the witnesses and their claims. He basically said, "I'll believe it when I see it for myself." But, once he beheld his risen Savior, as the others had already done, all doubts were satisfied. Why then, is the moniker *Doubting* forever linked to Thomas?

The companion account of this appearance by Jesus to His disciples can be found in Luke chapter 24. In verses 36–48, we see all the disciples are gathered together, perhaps Thomas was absent from this encounter, Luke makes no mention of it. They were talking to two other disciples,

Praying for Miracles

one named Cleopas who had just encountered the risen Christ on the road to Emmaus. In this passage Jesus calls all of them doubters:

> [36]While they were telling these things, He Himself stood in their midst and said to them, "Peace be to you."
> [37]But they were startled and frightened and thought that they were seeing a spirit.
> [38]And He said to them, "Why are you troubled, and why do doubts arise in your hearts?"
> [39]"See My hands and My feet, that it is I Myself; touch Me and see, for a spirit does not have flesh and bones as you see that I have."
> [40]And when He had said this, He showed them His hands and His feet.
> [41]While they still could not believe it because of their joy and amazement, He said to them, "Have you anything here to eat?"
> [42]They gave Him a piece of a broiled fish;
> [43]and He took it and ate it before them.
> [44]Now He said to them, "These are My words which I spoke to you while I was still with you, that all things which are written about Me in the Law of Moses and the Prophets and the Psalms must be fulfilled."
> [45]Then He opened their minds to understand the Scriptures,
> [46]and He said to them, "Thus it is written, that the Christ would suffer and rise again from the dead the third day,
> [47]and that repentance for forgiveness of sins would be proclaimed in His name to all the nations, beginning from Jerusalem.
> [48]"You are witnesses of these things."

So, based upon Luke's account, the disciples *all* failed to believe, and Jesus offered *all* of them the physical proof that would cure their unbelief. In this account, Jesus instructed them to touch His wounds as evidence that it was He in resurrected form. Again, no information is relayed as to whether or not any of them actually ventured forward and touched the wounds as Jesus offered for them to do. In this account, that is not the end of the story. They did not *then* rejoice. Nope, it says they still doubted. Luke 24:41–43 picks up the story:

> [41]While they still could not believe it because of their joy and amazement, He said to them, "Have you anything here to eat?"
> [42]They gave Him a piece of a broiled fish;
> [43]and He took it and ate it before them.

Faithful or Faithless?

The disciples were not ready to rejoice after seeing his wounds, this time they were offered additional proof in order for it to sink in. He even went a step further eating a piece of broiled fish, so they could see for sure that He was more than just an apparition of some form. So, without lecturing them for their lack of faith, or slapping the title *Doubting* in front of their names, Jesus offered the additional proof they needed to help them believe. But, even after ingesting a piece of fish in their presence the disciples were still lacking understanding about the resurrection. It isn't until verse 45–48 that Jesus actually got the point through to them by supernaturally opening their minds to understand:

> [45]Then He opened their minds to understand the Scriptures,
> [46]and He said to them, "Thus it is written, that the Christ would suffer and rise again from the dead the third day,
> [47]and that repentance for forgiveness of sins would be proclaimed in His name to all the nations, beginning from Jerusalem."
> [48]"You are witnesses of these things."

Jesus showed the disciples His wounds, then He ate a fish, and then He opened their minds to understand what Scripture had prophesied about Him. According to the account by Luke it took an awful lot to overcome the disciples doubting. Jesus knew they needed evidence and He willingly provided it to them. He suggested they touch him if they needed to, He ate fish to prove He was not just a spirit, and then He gave them an in-depth Bible study to clarify what they had witnessed.

Martin Luther goes on in his exposition of the account to say:

> These things are written for our sake, that we should learn how Christ loves us, and how friendly, paternally, kindly, and mildly he treats us, and will continue to treat us. It may be that he has retained the same signs and marks which perhaps will shine much brighter and more glorious than his whole body, and that he will exhibit them before the whole world, as the Scripture says, "They shall look upon him whom they have pierced." But that the Lord shows his hands and his feet, he thereby gives us to understand, that his works and no others belong to salvation, for by hands and feet the Scriptures understand the works and conduct.[2]

We all need evidence, not just the disciples, and certainly not just singling out poor Thomas. Luckily we have ours in the form of the written

---

2. Mueller, *Luther's Explanatory Notes on the Gospels*, 400.

Scriptures which capture all this evidence for us. It is also based upon the witness of those faithful believers who have gone before us, who so faithfully relayed their experiences to us. Like Hebrews 12:1 explains:

> "We have so great a cloud of witnesses surrounding us."

From this brief look at the passages relating to Thomas and his doubting, we see that he was in good company. For some reason, over the centuries Thomas had been singled out and labeled as the doubter of the bunch, because he asked for a miracle, because he asked for evidence. However, according to Jesus, they all were doubters who needed evidence to be convinced, and Christ was more than happy to offer it in order to build their faith. Interestingly, Jesus never preached a sermon at Thomas rebuking his lack of faith.

Christ did not label Thomas *Doubting Thomas* for requesting proof, and nor should we. Christ responded lovingly to Thomas, basically He was saying . . . There is no need to doubt anymore, you needed to see me, and here I am. The Lord simply added a special blessing to the believer's who would come after those first-hand eye witnesses like Thomas. In John 20:29 the Lord said, "Blessed are they who did not see, and yet believed." After reading the entire account in context, you realize that this verse was not comparing Thomas to the other ten disciples. All 11 disciples present had been offered the exact same physical proof, so they were all being referred to as those who *had seen and believed*. The story of His resurrection had obviously been told to other followers who had believed without the benefit of proof or a physical appearance from the Lord. I believe He was also talking about you and I, and the believers of our generation as well, when He blessed those who did not see and yet believed.

The disciples not only witnessed Jesus perform miracles during His ministry, they were empowered by Him to do the same. Remember that before His crucifixion and resurrection Jesus had sent them on a trial run of sorts. We find the story in Luke 9:1–6:

> [1]And He called the twelve together, and gave them power and authority over all the demons and to heal diseases.
> [2]And He sent them out to proclaim the kingdom of God and to perform healing.
> [3]And He said to them, "Take nothing for *your* journey, neither a staff, nor a bag, nor bread, nor money; and do not *even* have two tunics apiece.

> ⁴Whatever house you enter, stay there until you leave that city.
> ⁵And as for those who do not receive you, as you go out from that city, shake the dust off your feet as a testimony against them."

The disciples were given the power to perform miracles and heal the sick in preparation for the day they would be called to spread the Gospel to the uttermost parts of the world on their own. They were sent out to minister in His name, and given authority to perform miracles as proof of their message. Luke 9:6 says:

> ⁶Departing, they *began* going throughout the villages, preaching the gospel and healing everywhere.

When they got back, they gave a report to Him in Luke 9:10:

> ¹⁰When the apostles returned, they gave an account to Him of all that they had done. Taking them with Him, He withdrew by Himself to a city called Bethsaida.

The disciples came back from this life changing trip and immediately failed to live in the power they had been given. It was like selective amnesia came over the entire group and they simply forgot all the miracles they had just witnessed God do through them on their journey. (Sounds a lot like the way the Israelites forgot all they had seen God do.) When a large crowd that Jesus was teaching got hungry they just threw up their hands and felt helpless to meet the need, but clearly Jesus was trying to teach them that they could meet the need and continue to live in power and perform miracles. Luke 9:12–15 recounts the story:

> ¹²Now the day was ending, and the twelve came and said to Him, "Send the crowd away, that they may go into the surrounding villages and countryside and find lodging and get something to eat; for here we are in a desolate place."
> ¹³But He said to them, "You give them something to eat!" And they said, "We have no more than five loaves and two fish, unless perhaps we go and buy food for all these people."
> ¹⁴For there were about five thousand men. And He said to His disciples, "Have them sit down *to eat* in groups of about fifty each."
> ¹⁵They did so, and had them all sit down.

As Christians we have been provided with the Scripture as evidence, as well as the Holy Spirit's ongoing witness in our lives. God still works miracles today. He still intervenes in the lives of believers to build our faith and authenticate His message. Like the disciples, He expects us to live in the power of faith. God is not your lucky rabbit's foot that you can rub whenever you need a little faith. Then stick it back in your pocket until you need a little more. That is definitely not the message I am trying to relay. God doesn't interact that way.

Asking for evidence is not sin and does not make you immature in your faith. At times that is precisely how God chooses to bolster our faith. That is why the story of the Apostle Thomas is so important. God knows we need proof and is happy to supply it. We are not mere mortals without hope and without access to the throne of God Himself. The Holy Spirit lives within us and we are called, just like the men and women on the pages of Scripture to pray for God to be God and reveal Himself in powerful and yes, miraculous ways.

THOUGHT QUESTIONS CHAPTER 8

1. What have you been taught about Doubting Thomas in the past?
2. Have you ever studied the entire story in context before?
3. Why do you think Jesus chose to offer His hands and side as proof to the disciples?
4. How has studying Thomas' story in context changed your view of him?
5. What part did the miraculous play in this story? Name some of them.
6. What part does the miraculous play in your story?

9

God Honors Our Request for Fleeces

LET'S LOOK AT THE story of Gideon. Many of you have a very low opinion of poor Gideon as well. I can't blame you for that. You have been told all your life what a spiritual weakling he was. The story of Gideon and his infamous fleeces has served as a warning to you that only someone of little character and next to no backbone would ever dare test God by asking Him to perform a miracle. I hope to dismiss that fallacy. I believe Gideon's familiar story has also been removed far out of its context.

I know the mere title of this chapter is reason enough for some of you to get defensive. But before you put up your dukes, just take a moment to check out the passage for yourself, keeping an open mind. Gideon lived during the time of the judges and his story has been so twisted that we think of him in a bad light without batting an eyelash. But, if we explore his story in context, we might draw another conclusion entirely.

The phrase *don't pray for fleeces* has become so much a part of Christian orthodoxy that we confuse it with other pithy sayings, like those by Confucius found inside fortune cookies. Those sayings are not found in Scripture either, but we have heard them so often that we would swear by them. The matter of fact is that we are never commanded in Scripture to-*not pray for fleeces*. That interpretation and instruction has been added by teachers over the centuries. I think it is baseless. As we explore the story in Judges 6 and 7, I think you will be convinced of the falseness of this teaching as well.

The first thing to note is how incredibly similar the story in Judges 6 is to accounts in Genesis 17, 18 and 22, about Abraham's encounters with the Angel of the Lord. What happens to Gideon is a mirror reflection of a similar encounter by Abraham. Notice all the similarities:

God Honors Our Request for Fleeces

Abraham	Gideon
Under the oaks of Mamre	Under the oaks of Ophrah
The Angel of the Lord appeared to him	The Angel of the Lord appeared to him
Abram's name changed in Genesis 17:5	Gideon's name changed in Judges 6:32
Tested by God—to sacrifice Isaac	Tested by God—to tear down altars
Proved he trusted God and obeyed	Proved he trusted God and obeyed
Built an altar, named to honor God	Built an altar, named to honor God

Are all these similarities a mere coincidence? Why is Gideon tied so closely to the patriarch Abraham? Why does Scripture go to so much trouble linking the two men? I think it is because of the similarity of the two men in God's sight. It is a clear example of Gideon's faithfulness and his similarity to Abraham in that respect. Then why do we only know Gideon as a man of little faith, who offended God by asking for his miserable fleeces? Good question! Let's explore further.

The Lord had given Israel into the hand of Midian for seven years. The land was devastated, the people were despondent. But, when Israel finally cried out to God, He provided them with a deliverer, Gideon. When the Angel of the Lord first appeared to Gideon, he was hiding in a wine press, beating out wheat in hopes of hiding it from the Midianites. This is often called up as evidence that Gideon was a of low character. Does the fact that he was trying to hide wheat mean that Gideon had a personality flaw, or that he was a cowardly person? Not at all! Judges 6:3–5 gives us the background for his need to hide any wheat which he had managed to store:

> ³For it was when Israel had sown, that the Midianites would come up with the Amalekites and the sons of the east and go against them.
> ⁴So they would camp against them and destroy the produce of the earth as far as Gaza, and leave no sustenance in Israel as well as no sheep, ox, or donkey.

> ⁵For they would come up with their livestock and their tents, they would come in like locusts for number, both they and their camels were innumerable; and they came into the land to devastate it.

Simply put, Gideon was hungry! He was trying to save a little grain to eat. He was not any more afraid than anyone in else in Israel. Midian had done a thorough job of devastating the people and the land. These were desperate times. If he had any hopes of saving some of the wheat, he *had* to hide it. We pick up the story in Judges 6:11–14:

> ¹¹Then the angel of the Lord came and sat under the oak that was in Ophrah, which belonged to Joash the Abiezrite as his son Gideon was beating out wheat in the wine press in order to save it from the Midianites.
> ¹²The angel of the Lord appeared to him and said to him, "The Lord is with you, O valiant warrior."
> ¹³Then Gideon said to him, "O my lord, if the Lord is with us, why then has all this happened to us? And where are all His miracles which our fathers told us about, saying, 'Did not the Lord bring us up from Egypt?' But now the Lord has abandoned us and given us into the hand of Midian."
> ¹⁴The Lord looked at him and said, "Go in this your strength and deliver Israel from the hand of Midian. Have I not sent you?"

In Judges 6:12 we see God's greeting to Gideon. God calls him *O valiant warrior*. Whether that is who Gideon actually was at the time, or who he was destined to become, that is the way God saw Gideon—as a valiant warrior. How many other spiritual weaklings does God address as *O valiant warrior*?

Then in verse 13 Gideon responds by questioning Israel's circumstances. They felt abandoned by God. Gideon asks the Lord specifically:

> ¹³Then Gideon said to him, "O my lord, if the Lord is with us, why then has all this happened to us? And where are all His miracles which our fathers told us about, saying, 'Did not the Lord bring us up from Egypt?' But now the Lord has abandoned us and given us into the hand of Midian."

Gideon had yet to experience God's miracles, he had only heard about them. Gideon believed all that he had been told about God and His glorious miracles, even though he had not personally witnessed any in his lifetime. Does that sound like a man of little faith?

Notice too, the stylistic similarity of making a statement by way of using an interrogatory form. This is the same as God's query in verse 14, "Have I not sent you?" Gideon had never questioned whether or not he had been sent. In fact, he had just received the command to deliver Israel. He was directed by God to, "Go in this your strength and deliver Israel." Again, whether Gideon was strong at this point in the story or whether that is the way God viewed him, Gideon was noted by God for his strength.

Then God directly commissions Gideon to deliver the Israelites from Midian. Gideon responds as so many others had when God spoke directly to them, in disbelief and wondering why He would choose them for something so grand. Noah, Abraham, David, Moses and even the virgin Mary, all reacted the same way when first informed of God's call on their lives. You can't fault Gideon for questioning it. None of those others are condemned for questioning God's call, and being dumbfounded by God including them in His plan. That does not prove he is lacking faith. That proves he is human as well as humble. How do we expect him to respond? Should he have been arrogant and overly confident, "Oh well, I knew you would come sooner or later God. Of course you would pick me to lead the people. I never doubted it for a minute." God never chooses a John Wayne character to lead His people. Even King Saul was found hiding among the baggage before his anointing as the first king of Israel.

Gideon asks for a sign to prove that God was really who he was speaking to in verse 17. God happily obliges by consuming the offering with fire in Judges 6:21 where we read:

> [21]Then the angel of the Lord put out the end of the staff that was in his hand and touched the meat and the unleavened bread; and fire sprang up from the rock and consumed the meat and the unleavened bread. Then the angel of the Lord vanished from his sight.

No lightning bolts came crashing down due to his insolence. No rebuke for being disbelieving and asking God for a sign, just proof positive provided by way of a miracle, followed by reassurance that Gideon would not die after seeing the Lord. Whew! How many spiritual giants have actually been visited by the Lord? This puts Gideon in rare company with the patriarchs and even Moses. It's a very selective group.

Praying for Miracles

God tests Gideon to prove his faith, just like he tested Abraham to prove his. Gideon is asked to go tear down the altars the people had built to the idol Baal. In Judges 6:24–32 we read:

> [24]Then Gideon built an altar there to the Lord and named it The Lord is Peace. To this day it is still in Ophrah of the Abiezrites.
> [25]Now on the same night the Lord said to him, "Take your father's bull and a second bull seven years old, and pull down the altar of Baal which belongs to your father, and cut down the Asherah that is beside it;
> [26]and build an altar to the Lord your God on the top of this stronghold in an orderly manner, and take a second bull and offer a burnt offering with the wood of the Asherah which you shall cut down."
> [27]Then Gideon took ten men of his servants and did as the Lord had spoken to him; and because he was too afraid of his father's household and the men of the city to do it by day, he did it by night.
> [28]When the men of the city arose early in the morning, behold, the altar of Baal was torn down, and the Asherah which was beside it was cut down, and the second bull was offered on the altar which had been built.
> [29]They said to one another, "Who did this thing?" And when they searched about and inquired, they said, "Gideon the son of Joash did this thing."
> [30]Then the men of the city said to Joash, "Bring out your son, that he may die, for he has torn down the altar of Baal, and indeed, he has cut down the Asherah which was beside it."
> [31]But Joash said to all who stood against him, "Will you contend for Baal, or will you deliver him? Whoever will plead for him shall be put to death by morning. If he is a god, let him contend for himself, because someone has torn down his altar."
> [32]Therefore on that day he named him Jerubbaal, that is to say, "Let Baal contend against him," because he had torn down his altar."

In verse 27 we see Gideon's immediate response. No questions asked. He did it. I think too much is made of the fact that Gideon was too afraid to do it by day, so he chose to tear down the altars at night. It was a wiser choice not to ruffle the feathers of the men of the city as well as those of his father's house by waiting until broad daylight to carry out God's command. Notice that the command to tear the altars down came to Gideon *at night* according to verse 25. The very same night!

God Honors Our Request for Fleeces

He wasn't hiding out until the cover of darkness made him feel bold enough to carry out God's command as some have speculated. It was actually night time when the request was made. God commanded him to tear down the altar to Baal, and Gideon acted immediately. He didn't think it would be wise to do it in daylight, so he chose not to wait until daybreak. This detail actually verifies his faith and faithfulness. Gideon didn't question it, or take time to mull it over, or strategize to wait until it was dark outside the following night to perform what God had requested of him.

He simply chose not wait until daylight to carry out the command. God told him to do it, and it just so happened that it was already nighttime. Gideon didn't disobey God by *not waiting* until full daylight to tear down the altars. God never requested for him to wait until daytime to tear them down, just that he tear them down. The fact that Gideon even entertained doing so brash a thing in broad daylight actually shows his character. The fact that he decided that tearing down the altar by day would be unwise, just proves his wisdom and discernment.

His name is changed to Jerubbaal because of his faithfulness in carrying out God's command of tearing down the altar to Baal. If God had been disappointed with Gideon and the promptness of his actions, He may have postponed the changing of his name, or reprimanded Gideon for his fear. But, we see that God is prompt in his commendation as well.

Don't miss verse 34. It is key!

> [34]So the Spirit of the Lord came upon Gideon; and he blew a trumpet, and the Abiezrites were called together to follow him.

From this point on in the story Gideon did not act in his own human weakness, but is clothed with the Spirit of the Lord. In the Spirit he calls his army together. The section about the fleeces comes right on the heels of this, but rarely is that context exposited along with it. If you read the few verses about the fleeces (verses 36–40) out of context, it is no surprise you come up with a portrait of Gideon, the trembling, lily-livered leader, who needed signs for reassurance.

At face value, not taking any of the rest of the chapters before or after it into account, that is the impression you could get. I cannot believe how many preachers have so willingly taken these four little verses as a springboard for entire sermons about not asking for signs from God. But, in its proper context, these verses cannot support that conclusion. Gideon

Praying for Miracles

was clothed in the Spirit, and was acting in the Spirit, when he requested verification of God's plan. You can't get around that fact!

After being clothed in the Spirit and summoning his army together, Gideon then asks God to verify his marching orders. Gideon is not questioning God or *testing* Him. He is going bravely into battle and wants to make sure to consult the commander of his army, God Himself. That is something many of Israel's kings and commanders somehow overlooked at crucial times in their history, and they paid the price for it. Gideon doesn't make that same mistake, and refuses to go off half-cocked into battle and risk the slaughter of God's army. The others could have taken an important tip from Gideon's playbook. His humility does not equate to a character flaw. The Oxford Bible Commentary notices that humility is a key component of other Biblical heroes as well:

> Gideon requests and receives again a sign of YHWH's support. The symbol chosen, a fleece of wool, is drawn from the agricultural world that defines the Israelite community for many of the traditions in Judges, while the evidence of God's presence and power involves the deity's capacity to control and alter the normal course of nature. The hero's repeated request for a sign recalls Moses and more generally is a favorite biblical motif of the hesitant or insecure hero. Indeed YHWH favors those who are aware of their own weaknesses.[1]

Gideon should be commended instead of condemned for making sure he was on the same page with God, before taking the 32,000 Israelites down to be slaughtered by the Midianites and Amalekites. Gideon just wanted to double-check and make sure that he had heard the Lord correctly, and knew his marching orders. In retrospect that was a good call. Judges 6:36–40 says:

> [36]Then Gideon said to God, "If You will deliver Israel through me, as You have spoken,
> [37]behold, I will put a fleece of wool on the threshing floor. If there is dew on the fleece only, and it is dry on all the ground, then I will know that You will deliver Israel through me, as You have spoken."
> [38]And it was so. When he arose early the next morning and squeezed the fleece, he drained the dew from the fleece, a bowl full of water.

---

1. Nidich, "Judges," 182.

God Honors Our Request for Fleeces

³⁹Then Gideon said to God, "Do not let Your anger burn against me that I may speak once more; please let me make a test once more with the fleece, let it now be dry only on the fleece, and let there be dew on all the ground."

⁴⁰God did so that night; for it was dry only on the fleece, and dew was on all the ground.

Gideon first asks for God to make the fleece wet and the ground dry. Then, he asked once more to be 100 percent sure it had not been a fluke or just the result of natural causes simply creating dew on the fleece overnight. He requested that the fleece would be dry and the ground wet—a more definitive sign. God's response in verse 40 tells a lot, "*God did so that night* for it was dry only on the fleece, and dew was on all the ground."

God affirmed Gideon's leadership and affirmed the message He had given. God used the miracles to communicate clearly with Gideon. Gideon had heard that He was a God of miracles from his youth, he stated that in their first encounter, and so Gideon expected God to communicate in that way. Perhaps we are so far removed from that kind of faith, that expecting God to perform miracles and communicate through such means is completely foreign to us. Even though Gideon had not personally experienced God in this way, he had heard the stories and had been taught about his wonder-working God. That doesn't make his request wrong!

Some say that Gideon should have believed the Lord and never asked for the proof of the fleeces. I say, Gideon *did* believe the Lord, and that is exactly *why* he asked for the fleeces. He knew he was in charge and taking the very lives of his army of 32,000 men into his hands and wanted to get things right. Gideon didn't want to go off to battle without the assurance that it was God's plan. Gideon, clothed in the Spirit, wanted to wait patiently on the Lord for direction. He wasn't clothed in his own weakness, immaturity, or fear. He was clothed in the Spirit when he requested for God to communicate through miracles with the fleeces.

Take a look at the next chapter. We find more contextual clues here. In Judges Chapter 7, God delivers the Israelites in a miraculous way. This miracle of delivering the nation with only 300 men against armies as numerous as locusts and with innumerable camels was entirely God's idea. Gideon did not request this miracle. It was entirely God's design. Who would have imagined it? Back in Judges 6:5 we are told how many men they were attacking:

> ⁵For they would come up with their livestock and their tents, they would come in like locusts for number, both they and their camels were innumerable; and they came into the land to devastate it.

God decided that the people needed to see His power and be persuaded by a miracle to follow Him as their one true God once again. Like Gideon, this entire generation had only heard tales of their powerful, wonder-working God, and it was time for them to experience His power for themselves. God chose to get His people's attention in a miraculous way. We see that God was afraid they would be boastful if they took too many men, and might think that they had somehow defeated their enemies on their own, and in their own strength. Judges 7:2 reads:

> ²The Lord said to Gideon, "The people who are with you are too many for Me to give Midian into their hands, for Israel would become boastful, saying, 'My own power has delivered me.'"

So, God whittled down Gideon's army to a meager 300 men. God delivered them with only 300 men to make it clear that He had delivered them by a miracle that only He could be responsible for. God knew the hard hearts of the people He was dealing with, and wanted to make sure He got full credit for their deliverance. He wanted to leave no room for mistake, it was a miracle.

After sending the rest of the men home (those who were afraid and those who knelt to drink the water) God provided for Gideon's fear before battle. God anticipated the need for reassurance and provided it without being asked. This is very much like the way Jesus anticipated the need the disciples (including Thomas) would have to see his hands and his side and offered that proof to them without being asked.

God had an Amalekite soldier have a dream the night before battle, and allowed Gideon to hear about the prophecy of Israel's victory. We do not hear any rebuke from God at this point either. There is no *ye of little faith* condemnation. That misinterpreted note has been added by men over time. In his *Systematic Theology*, Lewis Sperry Chafer acknowledges God's use of signs to guide and legitimate His ambassadors, almost like supplying them with special credentials:

> God gave Gideon a sign in the camp of the Midianites of the victory which he should win (Judges 7:9–15), though it does not happen that the word occurs in that narration. Or it is possible for a man, under a strong conviction that the hand of God is leading

him, to set such and such a contingent event as a sign to himself, the falling out of which in this way or in that he will accept as an intimation from God of what He would have him do. Examples of this are not uncommon in Scriptures (Gen. 24:16; Judges 6:36–40; I Sam. 14:8–13).[2]

If that in-depth study of the passage, in its context, is not enough to convince you that Gideon was not in error for asking God to be God and perform miracles for him, and in the midst of His people Israel, then take a look at Hebrews 11:32. Here you find Gideon, in the company of a list of Old Testament faithful. He is listed in the same breath as five other heroes of the faith, Barak, Samson, Jephthah, David and Samuel. That's pretty good company. If the writer of Hebrews places Gideon in that prestigious list, why have modern preachers maligned his reputation and called him a spiritual weakling for so long? Give Gideon some credit, Scripture sure does. He was faith*ful*, not faith*less*; and test*ed*, not test*ing*. It took faith to tear down the idols of Baal. It took faith to ask for the miracles of the fleeces. It took faith to go into battle with only 300 men, a miracle he never would have asked for on his own. God honored Gideon and his request for reassurance in the fleeces and clothed him in the Spirit.

Now to be sure, his life ended poorly, just as King Solomon's would later, as well. His golden ephod became a snare for Israel as well as his own family. They began worshiping it like an idol and just after his death the nation went right back to worshipping the idols of Baal. At the end of Judges chapter 8:28–35, we find the sad end of Gideon's story:

> [28] So Midian was subdued before the sons of Israel, and they did not lift up their heads anymore. And the land was undisturbed for forty years in the days of Gideon.
> [29] Then Jerubbaal the son of Joash went and lived in his own house.
> [30] Now Gideon had seventy sons who were his direct descendants, for he had many wives.
> [31] His concubine who was in Shechem also bore him a son, and he named him Abimelech.
> [32] And Gideon the son of Joash died at a ripe old age and was buried in the tomb of his father Joash, in Ophrah of the Abiezrites.
> [33] Then it came about, as soon as Gideon was dead, that the sons of Israel again played the harlot with the Baals, and made Baal-berith their god.

---

2. Chafer, *Systematic Theology*, 175.

> ³⁴Thus the sons of Israel did not remember the Lord their God, who had delivered them from the hands of all their enemies on every side;
> ³⁵nor did they show kindness to the household of Jerubbaal (that is, Gideon) in accord with all the good that he had done to Israel.

Just like Solomon, Gideon had many offspring by many wives and concubines. And just like Solomon's son Rehoboam who ruled after him, Abimelech one of Gideon's sons was evil in God's sight. But, none of that was due to his asking for fleeces. Gideon's other character flaws may have taken him out in the end, but it had nothing to do with his asking God for the miracle of the fleeces. For a brief, shining moment, Gideon was a hero of the faith. And, although Gideon did not finish his life well, he was included in that illustrious group in the book of Hebrews, specifically because he had faith enough to ask for and trust God for miracles.

THOUGHT QUESTIONS FOR CHAPTER 9

1. What have you been taught about Gideon and his praying for fleeces?
2. Have you ever prayed for God to communicate with you in a similar way? How did God respond?
3. Gideon was clothed with the Spirit. What is our relationship to the Spirit as Christians today?
4. How does praying for miracles show how Gideon expected God to communicate with him?
5. How does God communicate with you?
6. Even though Gideon's life did not end well, what do you think about his leadership and God's calling on his life?

SECTION III

God's Communication Style

10

God Chooses to Use Miracles, Signs, and Wonders

GOD REVEALS HIMSELF THROUGH miracles, signs and wonders. They authenticate His presence, His message, and often His chosen messengers. The Old Testament is rife with examples. (Thomas Jefferson would have very little left, if he cut out all the miracles found in the Old Testament.) You might say that miracles, signs and wonders are the calling cards God chooses to leave behind to make sure you know where to send your thank you note. It is like a graffiti message painted on the side of a building saying, "God was here!"

One key example is found in the story of the Exodus. When God worked miracles on behalf of His people Israel, in procuring their safe departure out of Egypt. He did so to vindicate His glorious name. God sent His chosen messenger, Moses, to the Pharaoh of Egypt with His chosen message. In Exodus 5:1 it says:

> [1]And afterward Moses and Aaron came and said to Pharaoh, "Thus says the Lord, the God of Israel, 'Let My people go that they may celebrate a feast to Me in the wilderness.'"

Well, we are all familiar with Pharaoh's hard-hearted response to God's request. Not only did he continue to ignore Moses (and God) but he made life even harder for the Israelite slaves. So, God sent Pharaoh ten specific signs (or plagues) to authenticate Moses' message. But Pharaoh, believing himself to be a god, refused to relent. Wave after wave of disasters came upon Egypt and its stubborn ruler as a result. God chose to use miracles to get Pharaoh's attention and to ultimately free his people from slavery.

After the final plague where God slew all the first-born in Egypt, but passed over the homes of the Israelites, sparing their first-born because of the blood of the sacrifice painted on their doorposts, Pharaoh finally gave in. Pharaoh's own first-born son was sacrificed in an effort to maintain his stiff-necked arrogance. God used marvelous and amazing events to get Pharaoh's attention, and He still gets man's attention by miracles today.

But, don't forget that God used those same miracles to inspire the faith of His people as well. They would need a strong faith to make it through the desert and on to the Promised Land. In fact, the stories of God's amazing miracles are integral to the Jewish faith and are the backbone of our Christian faith. Most, if not all, of the Jewish Feasts and Festivals are in connection with a command to commemorate God's awesome and miraculous deeds.

Another amazing account of God revealing Himself through wonders is found in 1 Kings chapter 18. We are presented with the story of Elijah versus the prophets of Baal. During the reign of King Ahab, the true prophets of God had been either killed or exiled because the people did not want to hear from them. Israel preferred to worship the idol Baal instead and had chosen to listen to the prophets of this idol. The nation had rebelled against God from the leaders, King Ahab and Queen Jezebel, on down.

The prophet Elijah called for a show-down between God and the idol Baal at Mount Carmel. So he called the entire nation to join him there along with all the prophets of the idol Baal. In 1 Kings 18:22 we learn:

> [22]Then Elijah said to the people, "I alone am left a prophet of the Lord, but Baal's prophets are 450 men."

At first glance that doesn't sound like a fair fight, since Elijah was so vastly outnumbered. He challenged these false prophets to a sort of duel. They were both to build an altar and prepare an offering and they were to call on the name of their god to consume the offering in their presence with fire. The prophets of Baal took their turn first.

Verses 26–29 say that the prophets of Baal called on the name of their god from morning until noon and got no reply:

> [26]Then they took the ox which was given them and they prepared it and called on the name of Baal from morning until noon saying, "O Baal, answer us." But there was no voice and no one answered. And they leaped about the altar which they made.
> [27]It came about at noon, that Elijah mocked them and said, "Call out with a loud voice, for he is a god; either he is occupied or gone aside, or is on a journey, or perhaps he is asleep and needs to be awakened."
> [28]So they cried with a loud voice and cut themselves according to their custom with swords and lances until the blood gushed out on them.
> [29]When midday was past, they raved until the time of the offering of the evening sacrifice; but there was no voice, no one answered, and no one paid attention.

They yelled for him, they jumped around the altar, they cut themselves, and they raved. But, there was still no answer from the idol. Just a deafening silence from an inanimate object in which they had chosen to put all their faith.

Next it was Elijah's turn to call on the one true God and time for God to appear in the form of a miracle in the people's sight. After preparing his altar, Elijah even went a step further, and dug a trench around it, and poured jars of water all over it, saturating the wood, making it humanly impossible to light on fire. We read in verses 36–39 how God responded to Elijah:

> [36]At the time of the offering of the evening sacrifice, Elijah the prophet came near and said, "O Lord, the God of Abraham, Isaac and Israel, today let it be known that You are God in Israel and that I am Your servant and I have done all these things at Your word."
> [37]"Answer me, O Lord, answer me, that this people may know that You, O Lord, are God, and that You have turned their heart back again."
> [38]Then the fire of the Lord fell and consumed the burnt offering and the wood and the stones and the dust, and licked up the water that was in the trench.
> [39]When all the people saw it, they fell on their faces; and they said, "The Lord, He is God; the Lord, He is God."

God completely consumed the offering with fire and the people responded to the miracle by falling on their faces and worshipping the Lord.

Praying for Miracles

It is important to note that Elijah was not reprimanded by God for requesting Him to perform a miracle. God was more than happy to blow His competition away by performing an unexplainable act, by stepping out of Heaven and doing something truly wondrous for His people. God was not *offended* by the test, He was willing to vindicate His name and point to His own glory.

God chose to validate the ministry of His messenger Elijah, and vindicate Himself as the one true God, by performing an awesome miracle in front of the nation of Israel. God used miracles throughout the Old Testament in the same way. He is a God who is quite capable of stepping into our natural world and silencing His critics by signs and wonders.

One other example turned an Old Testament nay-sayer into a true believer. It is the story of King Nebuchadnezzar. He ruled Babylon during the time of Daniel's prophesy. His story picks up in Daniel chapter 4, where the great king recounts in verses 2–3:

> [2]"It has seemed good to me to declare the signs and wonders which the Most High God has done for me."
> [3]"How great are His signs and how mighty are His wonders! His kingdom is an everlasting kingdom and His dominion is from generation to generation."

But, Nebuchadnezzar didn't always feel that way. It took a lot to get his attention, and even more for the Babylonian king to bow in humility before God. The story of Daniel chapter four tells of a dream or vision that came to the king in the night, and the only one who could accurately interpret it for him was his servant, the exiled Jew, Daniel.

It was foretold that the king would be humbled and lose his senses for a time, even eat grass like a common animal. A year after the prediction, while King Nebuchadnezzar was marveling at his vast empire and his own glory and majesty, God revealed an awesome act of His sovereignty by taking it all away from the king. Daniel 4:30–32 states:

> [30]The king reflected and said, "Is this not Babylon the great, which I myself have built as a royal residence by the might of my power and for the glory of my majesty?"
> [31]While the word was in the king's mouth, a voice came from heaven, saying, "King Nebuchadnezzar, to you it is declared: sovereignty has been removed from you,
> [32]and you will be driven away from mankind, and your dwelling place will be with the beasts of the field. You will be given grass to

eat like cattle, and seven periods of time will pass over you until you recognize that the Most High is ruler over the realm of mankind and bestows it on whomever He wishes."

God was not willing to share His *glory* with anyone, not even a mighty king like Nebuchadnezzar. All that God said He would do, He did! And, at the end of seven years of insanity the king was restored and praised God in humility. Some scholars have dismissed this as a form of psychosis that was completely natural in its origins. But, even if the malady is explainable by science, the fact of its prediction one year prior to its occurrence speaks highly for divine intervention. It is impossible to predict a psychotic break before it actually occurs. Plus, the fact that Nebuchadnezzar, himself, acknowledged that God had performed a miracle in his life cannot be dismissed. The man who actually lived through these amazing events gave complete credit for it to God.

God chose to get a hold of King Nebuchadnezzar's heart by humbling him in a miraculous way. The king goes on to praise God in verse 37:

> [37]"Now I, Nebuchadnezzar, praise, exalt and honor the King of heaven, for all His works are true and His ways just, and He is able to humble those who walk in pride."

These are just a few brief samples of how God worked in miraculous ways in the Old Testament. There are countless others. In fact, as I stated earlier, you would be hard pressed to have anything left if you removed all the miracles from the Old Testament. They are God's hallmark, and scream of His glory.

Now let's take a look at some of the miracles in the New Testament. As we have seen, miracles prove that God is God. That is why Jesus employed them throughout His earthly ministry. They proved that He was God and was capable of miraculous works that only God could do. In John 14:11 Jesus said:

> [11]"Believe Me that I am in the Father and the Father is in Me; otherwise believe because of the works themselves."

That is an astounding statement. The miracles Jesus performed were for the sole purpose of drawing people into correct understanding of *who* He was and *what* His purpose was. Jesus said that no matter how deep a person's faith in Him was, He was willing to accept them and meet them right where they were. In other words, if you aren't strong enough to believe in Me based upon what I have told you (or literally take My word for it) then rely on the miracles you have seen Me do, they verify what I am telling you about *who* I am! Either way there is no room for unbelief.

Even skeptics like the Pharisees and Sadducees recognized that Jesus was capable of performing miracles. Not even those who hated Him denied the fact that miracles were taking place. We find accounts in both Matthew chapter 12 and Luke chapter 11 of the religious elite attributing the miracles Jesus performed as coming from Satan rather than God. Matthew 12:22–24 recounts:

> [22]Then a demon-possessed man who was blind and mute was brought to Jesus, and He healed him, so that the mute man spoke and saw.
> [23]All the crowds were amazed, and were saying, "This man cannot be the Son of David, can he?"
> [24]But when the Pharisees heard this, they said, "This man casts out demons only by Beelzebul the ruler of the demons."

They did not dispute the fact that miracles had taken place or that demons had been cast out. They couldn't. They just refused to believe that Christ was performing them as validation of His Messianic ministry. In Luke 11:14–16, it goes on to add one more detail. The motive of the Pharisees was to *test* Him in order to prove Him false:

> [14]And He was casting out a demon, and it was mute; when the demon had gone out, the mute man spoke; and the crowds were amazed.
> [15]But some of them said, "He casts out demons by Beelzebul, the ruler of the demons."
> [16]Others, to *test* Him, were demanding of Him a sign from heaven.

He had just performed a miracle and yet they requested something more amazing. They just wanted to test Him.

On the other hand, Christ was not offended by those who requested a sign, as long as it was with pure motives. When someone came to Him for healing, it was not because they lacked faith, rather it was because they had faith in the proper source. They knew in their heart that Christ was capable of performing miracles on their behalf, even when they approached Him humbly or timidly. Christ did not scold people for believing in Him based upon a miracle. Why do we admonish people for it today? God can take little faith and grow it, just like a tiny mustard seed grows into an giant plant.

Remember the story of the woman with the issue of blood in Mark 5:24–34? Although we don't know exactly what her ailment might have been, we know that it made her an outcast, since according to Jewish law touching blood made you impure and unclean. The woman had dealt with some form of hemorrhage for twelve years and yet had so much faith that she knew if she merely touched Jesus' garment, she would be healed. Verse 29 says:

> ²⁹Immediately the flow of her blood was dried up; and she felt in her body that she was healed of her affliction.

When Jesus felt that power had gone out from Him, He asked who had touched Him. When the woman fell down before Him and explained, Christ did not rebuke her for seeking to be healed. Instead He commends her for her faith in 5:34.

> ³⁴And He said to her, "Daughter, your faith has made you well; go in peace and be healed of your affliction."

Jesus acknowledged that her faith was in Him and in His power. He did not belittle her for expecting a miracle. He praised her for it. Just like our friends, Peter, Thomas and Gideon who asked God for a miracle, this woman expected God to perform a miracle and heal her. For some reason we don't condemn her for it, like we do the others. I've never understood that double-standard. It seems this woman gets a pass for expecting a sign, unlike the others we tend to vilify. Just as the miracles Jesus performed testified about who He was, the faithful who sought His miracles testified about the faith they possessed.

Now this was certainly not the response the unbelieving Pharisees got when they sought a sign. There is an incredible difference between asking for a sign in an attempt to verify what you know to be true and based upon faith in the right source, versus asking for a sign with the motive of tripping Him up or proving Him to be false. Jesus responds very differently when presented with these two very different motivations. But clearly, the woman who touched His garment to be healed, was praised for her faith and not chastised for seeking a miracle. There are many other examples like this in each of the Gospel accounts.

Praying for Miracles

Read the account of the Canaanite woman who requested Jesus to perform a miracle in Matthew 15:21–28:

> [21]Jesus went away from there, and withdrew into the district of Tyre and Sidon.
> [22]And a Canaanite woman from that region came out and began to cry out, saying, "Have mercy on me, Lord, Son of David; my daughter is cruelly demon-possessed."
> [23]But He did not answer her a word. And His disciples came and implored Him, saying, "Send her away, because she keeps shouting at us."
> [24]But He answered and said, "I was sent only to the lost sheep of the house of Israel."
> [25]But she came and began to bow down before Him, saying, "Lord, help me!"
> [26]And He answered and said, "It is not good to take the children's bread and throw it to the dogs."
> [27]But she said, "Yes, Lord; but even the dogs feed on the crumbs which fall from their masters' table."
> [28]Then Jesus said to her, "O woman, your faith is great; it shall be done for you as you wish." And her daughter was healed at once.

Here we read the story of a Canaanite woman who begged for Jesus to heal her daughter. Jesus never rebuked her for requesting Him to perform this miracle. He only said that he had come to the Jews first, but impressed by the amount of her persistence and her faith, performed the miracle for her as she had requested.

The signs and wonders that Jesus performed during His earthly ministry were crucially important. In John 10:25 He states:

> [25]Jesus answered them, "I told you, and you do not believe; the works that I do in My Father's name, these testify of Me."

The signs were performed to prove His message and validate His Messianic ministry. Later in John 15:22–24 Jesus restates that fact this way:

> [22]"If I had not come and spoken to them, they would not have sin, but now they have no excuse for their sin."
> [23]"He who hates Me hates My Father also."
> [24]"If I had not done among them the works which no one else did, they would not have sin; but now they have both seen and hated Me and My Father as well."

God Chooses to Use Miracles, Signs, and Wonders

    In the Old Testament, miracles proved the presence and provision of God. In the New Testament, we see that Christ embodied that very presence and provision among men. His miracles were like neon signs pointing to Himself as Messiah. These are just a few examples of how and why God used miracles in both the Old and New Testaments. Miracles, signs and wonders serve to validate the minister as well as the message. God takes out His personal rubber stamp and approves them leaving the witnesses in awe and without excuse for disbelief.

THOUGHT QUESTIONS FOR CHAPTER 10

1. Why did God choose to use ten precise miracles to display His power to Pharaoh? How does that relate to the ten commandments He would give his people in the near future?

2. Why had the Israelites begun to worship a physical idol like Baal, rather than their own God? How important was it for them to see God work in miraculous ways?

3. King Nebuchadnezzar needed to acquire some humility before bowing down to God? In what ways has God chosen to humble you?

4. How much faith does it take to believe in Christ? Why was it okay with Him for people to believe in Him based solely on His miracles?

5. How did the woman with the issue of blood show her great faith?

6. Why was Christ impressed by the faith of the Canaanite woman?

11

The True Meaning of Faith

MIRACLES ARE NOT POSSIBLE apart from a right relationship to God. Great faith does not produce them. Faith in and of itself is meaningless. The only thing that truly matters is *who* we are placing our faith in. Some people wrongly place their faith in their own faith. So, it is important to clarify terms at this point to be sure you know what I mean by faith.

St. Thomas Aquinas believed whole heartedly in miracles, and spoke often of them in his writings. He stated:

> The working of miracles is ascribed to faith for two reasons. First, because it is directed to the confirmation of faith; secondly, because it proceeds from God's omnipotence upon which faith lies. Nevertheless, just as besides the grace of faith, the grace of the word is necessary that people may be instructed in the faith, so too is the grace of miracles necessary that people may be confirmed in their faith.[1]

Faith is an integral part of who we are as Christians. Faith is also a necessary ingredient of believing in miracles. We know that we have been saved *by grace through faith* as it says in Ephesians 2:8. But, what does that really mean?

If I asked you to define faith, some of you might say that it means a child-like faith, in that we should not ask questions, but simply be able to believe like innocent children. I think this idea comes from the passage in Matthew 18:1–4:

---

1. Aquinas, *Summa Theologica*, 95.

Praying for Miracles

> ^{1}At that time the disciples came to Jesus and said, "Who then is greatest in the kingdom of heaven?"
> ^{2}And He called a child to Himself and set him before them,
> ^{3}and said, "Truly I say to you, unless you are converted and become like children, you will not enter the kingdom of heaven.
> ^{4}Whoever then humbles himself as this child, he is the greatest in the kingdom of heaven."

This is yet another passage which means something entirely different when read in its original context. It is not referring to a supposed *child-like faith* at all. It is an example of true *humility* when Jesus presents a child to his disciples and uses that child to teach them about humility. Just because children are often less cynical and more trusting than adults, doesn't imply that we, as Christians, are called to an ignorant or uneducated faith. A so-called *child-like faith* is not what we are called to. In fact we are told to grow up and mature in our faith and leave childish things behind. So, both cannot be true. In Ephesians 4:14–16 we are called to grow up and stop being like children:

> ^{14}As a result, *we are no longer to be children*, tossed here and there by waves and carried about by every wind of doctrine, by the trickery of men, by craftiness in deceitful scheming;
> ^{15}but speaking the truth in love, we are to *grow up* in all aspects into Him who is the head, even Christ,
> ^{16}from whom the whole body, being fitted and held together by what every joint supplies, according to the proper working of each individual part, causes the growth of the body for the building up of itself in love.

Some of you might say it has to do with the idea of a *blind faith*. You might say we are called to believe in things that we cannot see with our own eyes, as if somehow we are to put on a blind-fold and stumble into our faith without the aid of our senses. But, we are never called to *blind-faith* either in Scripture. It is another one of those statements which has been said so often, people simply accept that it must be Biblical, but can't seem to put their finger on the precise verse. Our faith is not *blind*. It has a firm basis in reality. We are never called to believe in Christianity blindly or senselessly.

While still others might quote Hebrews 11:1 where it says, "Now faith is the assurance of things hoped for, the conviction of things not seen." This is the often quoted definition of faith. But where does that

The True Meaning of Faith

assurance come from and what is the basis for that conviction? Have you ever stopped to think about it? Our faith is not some ethereal, intangible idea. It has a basis in the evidence provided to us in Scripture and upon the reliable testimony of witnesses.

The kind of faith we mean has a definite object and focus—Christ Himself. Take for instance the classic trust exercise where a group of people bind their arms tightly together, and if you trust them to catch you, then you are willing to fall backward into their arms. Our faith in Christ is *not* like folding our arms across our chest and falling backward into the thin air of something called *faith,* hoping it might have the substance to break our expected fall. Rather, we are falling back into the trustworthy arms of our Savior, who is perfectly positioned and undoubtedly strong enough to catch us. See the difference? Our faith has substance.

In Charles C. Ryrie's, *So Great Salvation*, he digs deep into what it means to believe in Christ. In his explanation of what is meant by *faith*, he says:

> Trust, however, implies reliance, commitment, and confidence in the object or truths that one is trusting. An element of commitment must be present in trusting Christ for salvation, but it is commitment to Him, His promise, and His ability to give eternal life to those who believe.
>
> The object of faith or trust is the Lord Jesus Christ, however little or much one may know about Him. The issue about which we trust Him is His ability to forgive our sins and take us to heaven. And because He is the Lord God, there is an element in bowing before Him and acknowledging Him as the most superior Person when one trusts Him for salvation.[2]

The message of our faith might be that I don't believe in myself to *be* good enough to please God. I believe that Christ's sacrifice *was* good enough to please God. This is the crucial difference between Biblical Christianity and all other world religions. The miracle of God's grace was given to us through Jesus. All the work was accomplished by Him, so we deserve none of the credit. Like it says in Ephesians 2:8–10:

> [8]For by grace you have been saved through faith; and that not of yourselves, *it is* the gift of God;
> [9]not as a result of works, so that no one may boast.

---

2. Ryrie, *So Great Salvation*, 121.

> [10]For we are His workmanship, created in Christ Jesus for good works, which God prepared beforehand so that we would walk in them.

Every other religion relies on the good works of men to qualify them to enter a happy eternal state—heaven, nirvana, enlightenment—whatever they call it. There is some type of list that people need to check off. There are the good or desirable things they *should do*, along with a defined list of things that are morally or spiritually bad or undesirable, which they definitely *should not do*.

For example, Hinduism as well as Buddhism sees everything in cycles and your good or bad actions bring you either good or bad karma during your lifetime. Hopefully over the course of several lifetimes you might learn your karmic lesson, and your actions will become better and more desirable. In other words, your destiny hinges upon your good deeds.

Likewise, every Muslim must adhere to the five pillars of their faith and check each one off their list, including daily prayers and at least one journey to Mecca, in order to be a faithful Muslim. Your good deeds earn you God's favor.

Even some Catholics miss the point, and rely on counting up their gold stars in hopes that those will out-number their demerits in the end, rather than resting in the fact that Christ did *all* the work for them. Catholicism has its seven sacraments, which you *must* partake in, and seven deadly sins, which you *must* avoid at all costs. I know some Catholics who have failed in some area of keeping the list, and therefore they have given up all hope of redemption. I know others who have failed in some area, and although they are technically not qualified to, they take communion anyway in the hopes that their faithfulness in that regular act might tip the scales back in their favor.

This is the one primary aspect that sets Biblical Christianity apart from all other faiths. Salvation for the Christian is procured by what Jesus accomplished for us by His sacrificial death and miraculous resurrection, and not by what we do or do not do.

Our own works or good deeds do not save us. It is the belief that God's grace is enough to save us. Our salvation is based upon our acceptance of the gift of grace that has been offered to us. In order to be *saved* you must know and accept that you need a Savior. You are literally

The True Meaning of Faith

saved *from something*, eternal separation from God and punishment for sin. And, yes Virginia, there is a Hell.

Let's study Romans 4:1–8:

> ¹What then shall we say that Abraham, our forefather according to the flesh, has found?
> ²For if Abraham was justified by works, he has something to boast about, but not before God.
> ³For what does the Scripture say? "Abraham believed God, and it was *credited* to him as righteousness."
> ⁴Now to the one who works, his wage is not credited as a favor, but as what is due.
> ⁵But to the one who does not work, but believes in Him who justifies the ungodly, his faith is credited as righteousness,
> ⁶just as David also speaks of the blessing on the man to whom God credits righteousness apart from works:
> ⁷"Blessed are those whose lawless deeds have been forgiven, and whose sins have been covered.
> ⁸"Blessed is the man whose sin the Lord will not take into account."

Our justification is by faith rather than by works. Our righteousness is *credited* to us. It is not an earned wage. If we were paid the wage that we actually earned, we would be paid death and eternal separation from God. That is what our works have *earned* us. I don't want to cash that paycheck, do you? No amount of good deeds is enough to tip the scale in our favor.

The credit is not based on our ability to pay either, but on Christ's payment in full. We could never pass the credit check anyway, and we have no worthy collateral to offer up. You might think of it like a pre-paid gift card with a limitless balance to cover every sin we have committed or will ever commit. It has all been paid for in advance. Christ accepted our punishment, separation, and death. Your bill is stamped: debt paid in full.

You cannot believe in or pray to a God of miracles unless you first have put your faith in the right source. If you believe that God is who He says He is, then you can believe that God *will do* what He says He will do. Your belief or faith in God is credited as righteousness. It is your willingness (your commitment) to fall back into His strong arms. Not child-like or blindly, but soberly and willingly. Christ died as our substitute, taking all our punishment, and paying our debt in full. Christ rose from the dead to prove that we, too, will inherit eternal life through our reliance on His sacrifice. Romans 5:8–11 explains:

> ⁸But God demonstrates His own love toward us, in that while we were yet sinners, Christ died for us.
> ⁹Much more then, having now been justified by His blood, we shall be saved from the wrath of God through Him.
> ¹⁰For if while we were enemies we were reconciled to God through the death of His Son, much more, having been reconciled, we shall be saved by His life.
> ¹¹And not only this, but we also exult in God through our Lord Jesus Christ, through whom we have now received the reconciliation.

When someone gives you a gift, you don't have to pay them back for it. In fact, that would be considered rude. You wouldn't pull out your wallet and say to a friend, "Thanks for the gift, now what do I owe you?" All your friend wants you to do is open the package and enjoy the gift. That is the kind of faith we are talking about here. It is a willingness to accept a free gift, one we can never repay.

If we only received a free cup of coffee, then we feel that a simple thank you might suffice, but we just cannot fathom accepting something as costly as, say, a diamond ring with only a simple thank you. That is a stumbling block for many. Perhaps it has been a stumbling block for you, too. It is hard to take yourself and your own efforts out of the equation when discussing salvation. After all, you have had to work hard and earn everything your whole life. You have learned and accepted the statement that *nothing in life is free*. But just stop a moment and consider that if grace can be earned, then it is not grace at all! Grace is by definition receiving something that you did not deserve. While mercy on the other hand, is *not* receiving that which you *did* deserve, in our case death and eternal separation from a holy God.

It is only after we are saved through faith, that we can then act obediently in gratitude for the gift which we have received. Therefore, good deeds follow salvation, not the other way around. Good deeds to not lead to salvation.

What is in your heart? Do you have the humility of a child to accept the free gift that God gave to you? Or is your motivation to be in control of your own destiny, to pull yourself up by your own bootstraps, as it were? Do you feel the need to work hard and do good deeds in a futile effort to please God on your own terms? According to the Bible, God did not give you that option. You can either choose to present your works (good, bad, or indifferent) to God, or you can choose to present Christ's finished work (sacrificial death and resurrection) on your behalf. Are you ready to rest in the faith that God has done all the work for you in procuring your salvation and point to His completed work on the cross? Or are you just going to keep working on it yourself?

In Scripture we are told that there will be two different judgments. One is known as the Judgment Seat (or Bema) and the other is called the Great White Throne. You get to choose which one of these two judgments you want to stand before. The choice is yours!

The Judgment Seat is described in 1 Corinthians 3:10–15:

> [10] According to the grace of God which was given to me, like a wise master builder I laid a foundation, and another is building on it. But each man must be careful how he builds on it.
> [11] For no man can lay a foundation other than the one which is laid, which is Jesus Christ.
> [12] Now if any man builds on the foundation with gold, silver, precious stones, wood, hay, straw,
> [13] each man's work will become evident; for the day will show it because it is to be revealed with fire, and the fire itself will test the quality of each man's work.
> [14] If any man's work which he has built on it remains, he will receive a reward.
> [15] If any man's work is burned up, he will suffer loss; but he himself will be saved, yet so as through fire.

This judgment is reserved for the believer in Jesus. You notice that all the good works they do are actually built on top of the firm foundation of Jesus Christ. At this judgment, a person's deeds are tested with fire and only those deeds which are pleasing to God will remain. The rest of the deeds done with impure motives and those that do not please God will be entirely burned up.

The believer's works either receive reward or are counted as a loss. There is no mention of condemnation or any question of the believers themselves losing their salvation here. The person standing before this judgment is not in fear of punishment. It is all a matter of which deeds deserve a reward and which do not. The Bema Seat judgment is reserved for those who choose to trust in the free gift of salvation, which God has offered through Christ.

We can choose to be judged on the basis of accepting the gift of grace offered by Jesus' death (which provided full payment for our sin) and His resurrection (which passed along righteousness to believers). If we choose Christ, then the question of our eternal fate is settled prior to our judgment. It is only the deeds we do which might be lost, while others might merit a reward. There is no need for fear.

There is another judgment reserved for those who trust in their own good deeds to outweigh their bad deeds. This judgment is known as the Great White Throne. All of those people, of all faiths (many of whom are good, kind and sincere people), who work very hard checking off their list and trying, in their own strength, to please God on their own terms will find themselves standing before this judgment. We find it described in Revelation 20:11–15:

> [11]Then I saw a great white throne and Him who sat upon it, from whose presence earth and heaven fled away, and no place was found for them.
> [12]And I saw the dead, the great and the small, standing before the throne, and books were opened; and another book was opened, which is the book of life; and the dead were judged from the things which were written in the books, according to their deeds.
> [13]And the sea gave up the dead which were in it, and death and Hades gave up the dead which were in them; and they were judged, every one of them according to their deeds.
> [14]Then death and Hades were thrown into the lake of fire. This is the second death, the lake of fire.
> [15]And if anyone's name was not found written in the book of life, he was thrown into the lake of fire.

That sounds pretty grim and terrifying by contrast to the Bema Seat. But, there is good news here. We get to choose how we will be judged! We get to choose which judgment we want to stand before. Those who choose to work for their salvation will be condemned on that basis. If you want God to judge you based upon your own efforts, then God will let you have it your way, and judge you on that basis, according to your deeds. Remember you are not being judged by comparison to other sinful men, you are being judged in comparison to God's own righteousness and holiness, which is a standard you can never meet. Your good deeds don't compare! Without faith in Christ, all your deeds will earn you is eternity in the lake of fire.

God tells us in the Bible that our own good works and merits will never be acceptable to Him. He spells it out plainly in advance. There is no need for any guess-work, or hoping that your good deeds might surpass your bad deeds. The choice is yours. Either your name is written in the book of life or it's not! It is really that black and white, and really that final.

Christ is the basis and substance of our faith. Without the miracle of the resurrection, we are hopeless and helpless to save ourselves. That is the true definition of faith. Miracles are not based on how good we are, but to whom we are rightly related. Our faith does not work miracles. Miracles are God's business! Without a right relationship to God, praying for miracles is just a waste of your breath.

THOUGHT QUESTIONS FOR CHAPTER 11

1. How would you define faith?
2. Why is your faith a critical aspect to the whole idea of praying for miracles?
3. Who or what is your faith in? Christ alone or your own good deeds?
4. Describe the Bema Seat Judgment in your own words?
5. Describe the difference in the Great White Throne Judgment?
6. What do you deserve as wages? What have you been saved from?

12

How to Grow Your Mustard Seed

As we have discussed in previous chapters, I believe that God uses miracles, at times, to grow our faith. Every time we witness Him in His miraculous power, our trust and faith grows incrementally. This is a process I like to call *growing your mustard seed*.

Have you ever noticed that God spent years, even decades, developing and growing the faith of the people we find recorded in Scripture, before He called them to put that faith to the test? For example, Abraham was not called to sacrifice Isaac until after he had witnessed God's miracles over the course of decades. Abraham was asked to trust God and go to a new land. God prospered him all along the way.

Abraham was promised a son and God provided Isaac in his old age. There were so many experiences, and so many times, Abraham marveled at the God he served. The trust was developed and the relationship fostered. Only when the time was right, and only when God had grown Abraham's faith and adequately groomed him, was he told to sacrifice Isaac on an altar. That is the way God worked with the faithful men and women in the Bible. And, that is the way He works with us as well.

Another example that we touched on earlier was Peter walking on the water. The disciple, Peter, wasn't encouraged to step his foot out of the boat and walk to Christ on the sea the first day they met. On that first day, he was told to leave everything and follow Jesus. That, in and of itself, was a bold request. That first huge step of faith lead to all the others that followed. It led all the way up to Peter swinging his leg over the edge of a boat on a windy night and stepping onto the waters of Galilee.

Praying for Miracles

There was a track record and a trust, not to mention a deep relationship. His faith in Jesus had grown over time. He had seen Jesus perform many miracles and had witnessed enough to know that Jesus was the Son of God. Once Peter was convinced of that, and had a firm basis to believe that walking on the water was possible, once he believed that the Son of God could perform that kind of miracle—then he suggested that he was ready to give walking on water a try, then he followed through on his belief and stepped over the side of the boat.

In Matthew 17:20, Christ teaches His disciples how powerful their faith can be. Faith in the right source is able to tap them into God's miraculous power. When a possessed man is brought to Christ because the disciples were unable to heal him by themselves, Jesus didn't get angry that they would ask Him for a miracle, just that they didn't have enough faith to see the miracle come about on their own. In Matthew 17:20, He teaches His disciples the power of their faith, even if it is as tiny as a mustard seed:

> [20]And He said to them, "Because of the littleness of your faith; for truly I say to you, if you have faith the size of a mustard seed, you will say to this mountain, 'Move from here to there,' and it will move; and nothing will be impossible to you.

From this passage, we see that Jesus expected his followers to have faith and ask for miracles in His name. The awesome example He gave, proves that not only is it okay to ask for miracles, it is actually His expectation for His followers. Jesus is teaching us to ask for big things that only He can accomplish.

The mustard seed is one of the tiniest of all plant seeds, the size of a pinhead, and yet it is able to produce mustard plants that that can stand taller than a human being. You could get lost in a fully grown field of mustard plants. The point being that it's not the size of your faith that matters. Don't miss that. The size of your faith is not what is powerful. The size of your faith is not what causes the mountain to move. It is the *content* of your faith that makes all the difference. It is more precisely who your faith is focused on. It is the size of your God that counts—your belief and trust in a wonder-working God who is able to make the mountain move.

You grow your mustard seed each and every time you trust God to lead you. The size of your faith is directly linked to the times you can point to, that God has been faithful to you. In other words, it is experience-based.

It is part of the process of sanctification. This kind of faith is rooted and grown in your personal journey of trusting and obeying. I know it sounds redundant but, the more you trust and obey, the easier it becomes to trust and obey. And yes, God does allow for trials to enter your life in order that your faith would have a chance to grow.

If you really think about it, you would probably agree that some of the most difficult or painful times you have struggled through have also been the times of greatest growth in your faith. Funny how that works. When life is rolling along just fine, there is no reason to spend time on our knees. But, when everything is falling apart, there is no other place to turn.

In Joshua we read that the Israelites crossed over the Jordan River on dry land. Once they reached the other side, they were told to place stones to commemorate that miraculous provision of the Lord. The stones were there to remind them of His faithful deliverance and they were expected to teach their children and their children's children about what God had done for them on that very spot. Read Joshua 4:1–7:

> ¹Now when all the nation had finished crossing the Jordan, the Lord spoke to Joshua, saying,
> ²"Take for yourselves twelve men from the people, one man from each tribe,
> ³and command them, saying, 'Take up for yourselves twelve stones from here out of the middle of the Jordan, from the place where the priests' feet are standing firm, and carry them over with you and lay them down in the lodging place where you will lodge tonight.'"
> ⁴So Joshua called the twelve men whom he had appointed from the sons of Israel, one man from each tribe;
> ⁵and Joshua said to them, "Cross again to the ark of the Lord your God into the middle of the Jordan, and each of you take up a stone on his shoulder, according to the number of the tribes of the sons of Israel.
> ⁶Let this be a sign among you, so that when your children ask later, saying, 'What do these stones mean to you?'
> ⁷then you shall say to them, 'Because the waters of the Jordan were cut off before the ark of the covenant of the Lord; when it crossed the Jordan, the waters of the Jordan were cut off ' So these stones shall become a memorial to the sons of Israel forever."

Notice that the stones were actually taken from the bed of the river, that is why they were smooth. Every time they passed by that pile of smooth river rocks, the people would be reminded about where those stones came from. If there had never been a trial, in this case a river to cross, there would not have been the need for faith, or the opportunity for God to perform a miracle to provide for that need, nor a story to tell to coming generations.

Trials and obstacles are good things. They allow God to be awesome and meet our needs in miraculous ways. They also give us a chance to sit back and watch God fix our problems for us, rather than spinning our own wheels and trying to take care of it ourselves.

Throughout the life of any believer, we should litter our paths with smooth stones, so that those who come after us will be constantly reminded of God's miraculous work in our life. The hope is that every time you lack faith and turn around to backtrack where you have already been, you will stub your toe on one of those stones, and it will remind you of God's miracles and reinforce your faith. Your children and your children's children will find themselves tripping over all the stones you left in your wake, long after you are gone. That's my hope anyway!

Have you ever seen God's miraculous power? Do you have any smooth stones scattered along the path you have walked, reminding you of what God has done for you? Have you recounted those to your children and to your grand children? Maybe it is time to take an account of all the ways He has been faithful, and allow your mustard seed to grow.

What does faith look like when it is put into action? James 2:20–24 speaks of the union between our faith and our works (or actions), it reads:

> [20]But are you willing to recognize, you foolish fellow, that faith without works is useless?
> [21]Was not Abraham our father justified by works when he offered up Isaac his son on the altar?
> [22]You see that faith was working with his works, and as a result of the works, faith was perfected;
> [23]and the Scripture was fulfilled which says, "And Abraham believed God, and it was reckoned to him as righteousness," and he was called the friend of God.
> [24]You see that a man is justified by works and not by faith alone.

This is the other half of the equation. The knowing of a thing and the doing of it are joined. Just as someone who claims to believe one thing and yet does the opposite, proves themselves to be a hypocrite, their actions speak louder than their words. Our faith in God is proven by our actions, just like Abraham's head knowledge and his heart faith are indelibly linked to the faithful act of preparing the altar, binding his beloved son Isaac, and raising the dagger in his hand. His actions proved that what was in his head was actually what was in his heart. It proved that what he *said* was true, is actually what he *believed* to be true. Abraham believed that God was good for His word and able to work miracles, even able to bring Isaac back from the dead, if that was necessary. Do your driving habits justify the ichthus fish that is swimming across the back of your car? Do your actions prove what you believe to be true?

This passage, taken out of context, can be mistakenly interpreted as promoting a works-based theology. But, that is not the point James is making at all. He is merely teaching us that our actions do indeed speak louder than our words. What we speak with our mouth, where our feet step, or our hands touch, are the truest test of the faith that we profess to have in our heart. If you believe it, then you will act like it.

The entire chapter of Hebrews 11 is witness to this fact. It recounts a list of many of the Old Testament saints who had faith in God and trusted in Him for their salvation, rather than relying on their own good works to outweigh their bad. As we have seen, faith is defined in Hebrews verse 1:

> [1]Now faith is the assurance of things hoped for, the conviction of things not seen.

Our faith is literally proved by the good works we do. Check out the rest of Hebrews chapter 11. The entire chapter tells of what Old Testament saints did and how those actions or deeds, proved the faith they already had in God. Let's begin with a sample from verses 2–7:

> [2]For by it the men of old gained approval.
> [3]By faith we understand that the worlds were prepared by the word of God, so that what is seen was not made out of things which are visible.
> [4]By faith Abel offered to God a better sacrifice than Cain, through which he obtained the testimony that he was righteous, God testifying about his gifts, and through faith, though he is dead, he still speaks.
> [5]By faith Enoch was taken up so that he would not see death; and he was not found because God took him up; for he obtained the witness that before his being taken up he was pleasing to God.
> [6]And without faith it is impossible to please Him, for he who comes to God must believe that He is and that He is a rewarder of those who seek Him.

> [7]By faith Noah, being warned by God about things not yet seen, in reverence prepared an ark for the salvation of his household, by which he condemned the world, and became an heir of the righteousness which is according to faith.

Everything we see they did was in response to the God in whom they believed. It was not *what* they did, but *why* they did it, that God credited to them as righteousness. It was all about their hearts and their motives. The belief caused them to be righteous, the obedient deeds they did simply proved that their heart was in the right place, and that their true motivation was to please and praise God.

The rest of the chapter follows suit, reminding the reader of countless men and women who *by faith* were called righteous. After recounting example after example of Old Testament heroes of the faith whose deeds speak louder than words, the writer of Hebrews sums up his argument in chapter 11 with these words in verses 32–34:

> [32]And what more shall I say? For time will fail me if I tell of Gideon, Barak, Samson, Jephthah, of David and Samuel and the prophets, [33]who by faith conquered kingdoms, performed acts of righteousness, obtained promises, shut the mouths of lions,
> [34]quenched the power of fire, escaped the edge of the sword, from weakness were made strong, became mighty in war, put foreign armies to flight.

Each of these Old Testament characters were saved based upon their faith in God alone. Yet many of their faithful works or actions are recounted in this chapter to prove out the faith they claimed to believe.

What they actually did speaks volumes and testifies, or offers proof of what they believed and held to be true. But, it was not the action or works they performed that saved them, it was the faith they had in God alone. It was not based on the good things they did or the bad things they refrained from. The faith was the reason for the action. What each of them did and the faithful actions presented regarding them, simply prove their faith. Your actions prove what you believe to be true. What are your actions saying about what you believe?

You may notice, throughout the entire chapter, that quite a few of the actions listed for these heroes of the faith, were miracles, signs and wonders. But, I need to remind you, as I stated earlier, that God also allows for true calamity and trials of all kinds in the lives of believer's as well. God did not always provide for miracles to spare them from hardship or trials. He does not always provide for positive outcomes for His followers. You won't find any prosperity preaching here. Hebrews chapter 11 ends on a sour note in verses 35–40:

> [35]Women received back their dead by resurrection; and others were tortured, not accepting their release, so that they might obtain a better resurrection;
> [36]and others experienced mockings and scourgings, yes, also chains and imprisonment.
> [37]They were stoned, they were sawn in two, they were tempted, they were put to death with the sword; they went about in sheepskins, in goatskins, being destitute, afflicted, ill-treated
> [38](men of whom the world was not worthy), wandering in deserts and mountains and caves and holes in the ground.
> [39]And all these, having gained approval through their faith, did not receive what was promised,
> [40]because God had provided something better for us, so that apart from us they would not be made perfect.

Bad things do happen to good people. You can't get around that fact based on this passage. Although many of these Old Testament faithful did not ever see His promises fulfilled in their lifetimes, they still hoped in God's future provision. Don't lose sight of the fact that your belief in God's ability to perform miracles does not necessitate that His plan includes what you are praying for. We won't see all of our prayers answered in the affirmative, but we do have a firm hope that God has something better in store for us. Namely heaven!

I have heard stories of missionaries who spent their entire lives offering salvation to certain tribes without even one convert to show for their efforts. But, in the following generations, after the death of that missionary, their life's work bore fruit, and many were saved. Certainly those who were martyred by sword or saw, in the Hebrews passage, were not fervently in prayer for their own physical demise. That was not the miracle they were looking for, and yet that was God's plan for His glory.

The question remains: Do you believe that God is God and therefore capable of working miracles? Then, why don't your actions prove that out? Why do we ask for such mundane things, when He challenged us to ask for awesome signs and wonders? The bigger your view of God, the bigger your belief in His power.

Praying for Miracles

    Why do we only have faith enough to ask for God to remove the mole-hill in our way, when He is waiting with anticipation for us to request removal of the mountain? Do our prayers prove out the faith we claim to have, or does it prove us to be hypocrites, who talk a big game and fail to ask, seek and knock?

THOUGHT QUESTIONS FOR CHAPTER 12

1. How has God used circumstances to grow your mustard seed of faith?
2. What smooth stones do you have to point to about how God has shown Himself to be powerful and true in your life?
3. Whom do you need to share some of those stories with?
4. Why does God allow for trials and problems in our lives?
5. How have trials strengthened your faith, or grown your mustard seed?
6. Does your prayer life prove your belief in a wonder-working God?

13

Are Miracles Still Seen Today?

WE HAVE ALREADY EXPLORED the fact that miracles are not possible apart from a right relationship to God. Now we need to take up another powerful truth, miracles are not possible apart from the will of God either. No one can demand one like a spoiled child who stamps his foot and demands ice cream. God doesn't work that way.

You see, we can pray for things that we think fall into God's will, but we shouldn't be surprised when our fervent prayer is not answered in the manner we had hoped. God's plan for the healing of a friend or family member may not be the same as our plan in that situation. His will for our business, our relationships, as well as how our needs are met, may be far different from our will in those same areas.

Sometimes a spouse chooses to continue their affair and go forward with the divorce. Sometimes a child follows the call of their addiction rather than the call to come home to a loving family. Sometimes a friend or family member dies from the very disease that you have been praying God would take away. While we cannot see why or how any of those things could possibly be in the scope of God's will, we are simply not able to see the larger picture. As it says in Romans 11:33–36:

> [33]Oh, the depth of the riches both of the wisdom and knowledge of God! How unsearchable are His judgments and unfathomable His ways!
> [34]For who has known the mind of the Lord, or who became His counselor?
> [35]Or who has first given to Him that it might be paid back to Him again?

> ³⁶For from Him and through Him and to Him are all things. To Him be the glory forever. Amen.

Certainly, God's ways are not our ways. What you think is best is not always the best from God's vantage point. But, you can never go wrong in praying for His glory. That is, after all, the overarching theme that runs from Genesis to Revelation—God's own glory. When you pray for His glory in whatever circumstance, you can be assured that you are also praying for His will to be done.

1 Thessalonians 5:14–18 also expresses that peace within His church is part of God's will for us, and a part of that peace is *praying without ceasing*:

> ¹⁴We urge you, brethren, admonish the unruly, encourage the fainthearted, help the weak, be patient with everyone.
> ¹⁵See that no one repays another with evil for evil, but always seek after that which is good for one another and for all people.
> ¹⁶Rejoice always;
> ¹⁷*pray without ceasing*;
> ¹⁸in everything give thanks; for this is God's will for you in Christ Jesus.

Some confuse their will with God's will. Unfortunately some Christian churches teach that you would not have struggles if only your faith were big enough. We need to address this, because these churches and denominations actually blame the believer when they are not prospering, healthy, or happy. They teach that only the smallness of your faith allows all those problems to exist. In fact, if you just had *enough* faith, you would be prospering at every turn. You could be driving a Mercedes Benz, your illness would be healed, and your child would be on the straight and narrow path. Really?

That is just not sound teaching and it is a great distortion of this passage. When the body of Christ condemns its own members for some faulty perception (that if you are in the will of God, all your prayers will be answered in the positive), then they are just doing Satan's work for him. Condemnation is Satan's business, and not what the church should be about. Read Romans 8:1 over and over again, until it sinks in:

> ¹Therefore there is now no condemnation for those who are in Christ Jesus.

The disciples had questions in regards to suffering. Remember how Jesus corrected the disciples for the same faulty theology in John 9:1–3:

> ¹As He passed by, He saw a man blind from birth.
> ²And His disciples asked Him, "Rabbi, who sinned, this man or his parents, that he would be born blind?"
> ³Jesus answered, "It was neither that this man sinned, nor his parents; but it was so that the works of God might be displayed in him.

While the hardship you are facing might well be discipline to get you back on track. Your sin is not necessarily the cause of your troubles. It is not necessarily a form of punishment, as I believed for years suffering with migraine headaches. God could have simply allowed difficulties to arise *so that the works of God might be displayed in you.*

Ask God how His glory will be found in your circumstance. You might be surprised by the answer. It may not be in the solution that you have been praying for. It may not be in the miracle you have been waiting on. His glory may be seen simply in how you walk through the trial that you are facing. People are watching you, and waiting to see how you will react and how you will respond to that difficult situation in your path. The way you walk through it may be exactly how God gains glory from whatever you are dealing with. On the other hand, just as Jesus chose to heal the blind man so that the works of God might be displayed in him, God might decide to work a miracle in your situation. It all depends upon His will and what brings Him glory.

James 1:2–3, teaches that the amount of faith we have doesn't insulate us from various trials in life. In fact, God allows trials to test our faith and grow it even more. Trials and difficulties are not a sign of little faith, but a part of our training, whose ultimate goal is to produce endurance in our Christianity:

> ²Consider it all joy, my brethren, when you encounter various trials,
> ³knowing that the testing of your faith produces endurance.

Let me be very clear about this point. God is not your lucky rabbit's foot. He is never bound to fulfill your wishes and desires, no matter how fervently you pray for them. God's plan and your plan may not align for reasons that you may never know in this lifetime. The passage doesn't say *if* you encounter various trial, it says *when* you encounter various trials. Trials are not optional, or only reserved for those lacking faith. What we allow them to produce in our life is up to us.

Are Miracles Still Seen Today?

Remember, too, that not all the prayers of the Godly in the Bible were answered in the affirmative. David, the man after God's own heart, prayed diligently for God to spare his son as we read the story in 2 Samuel 12:13–23:

> [13]Then David said to Nathan, "I have sinned against the Lord." And Nathan said to David, "The Lord also has taken away your sin; you shall not die.
>
> [14]However, because by this deed you have given occasion to the enemies of the Lord to blaspheme, the child also that is born to you shall surely die."
>
> [15]So Nathan went to his house. Then the Lord struck the child that Uriah's widow bore to David, so that he was *very* sick.
>
> [16]David therefore inquired of God for the child; and David fasted and went and lay all night on the ground.
>
> [17]The elders of his household stood beside him in order to raise him up from the ground, but he was unwilling and would not eat food with them.
>
> [18]Then it happened on the seventh day that the child died. And the servants of David were afraid to tell him that the child was dead, for they said, "Behold, while the child was *still* alive, we spoke to him and he did not listen to our voice. How then can we tell him that the child is dead, since he might do himself harm!"
>
> [19]But when David saw that his servants were whispering together, David perceived that the child was dead; so David said to his servants, "Is the child dead?" And they said, "He is dead."
>
> [20]So David arose from the ground, washed, anointed himself, and changed his clothes; and he came into the house of the Lord and worshiped. Then he came to his own house, and when he requested, they set food before him and he ate.
>
> [21]Then his servants said to him, "What is this thing that you have done? While the child was alive, you fasted and wept; but when the child died, you arose and ate food."
>
> [22]He said, "While the child was *still* alive, I fasted and wept; for I said, 'Who knows, the Lord may be gracious to me, that the child may live.'
>
> [23]But now he has died; why should I fast? Can I bring him back again? I will go to him, but he will not return to me."

Or take for instance the Apostle Paul who served the Lord tirelessly after being converted on the road to Damascus. Paul was not relieved of a specific ailment, or *thorn in the flesh*, throughout his ministry. He prayed three times for its removal. A man who had the power to heal others,

Praying for Miracles

prayed for his own healing, but for some reason that request was denied. In 2 Corinthians 12:7–10 we read:

> ⁷Because of the surpassing greatness of the revelations, for this reason, to keep me from exalting myself, there was given me a *thorn in the flesh*, a messenger of Satan to torment me—to keep me from exalting myself!
> ⁸Concerning this I implored the Lord three times that it might leave me.
> ⁹And He has said to me, "My grace is sufficient for you, for power is perfected in weakness." Most gladly, therefore, I will rather boast about my weaknesses, so that the power of Christ may dwell in me.
> ¹⁰Therefore I am well content with weaknesses, with insults, with distresses, with persecutions, with difficulties, for Christ's sake; for when I am weak, then I am strong.

And Christ Himself had at least one prayer that God the Father refused to grant to Him. When He prayed in the Garden of Gethsemane, Jesus asked if there was any other way to accomplish salvation apart from the gruesome and torturous death that He was about to endure. In Mark 14:32–36 we find:

> ³²They came to a place named Gethsemane; and He said to His disciples, "Sit here until I have prayed."
> ³³And He took with Him Peter and James and John, and began to be very distressed and troubled.
> ³⁴And He said to them, "My soul is deeply grieved to the point of death; remain here and keep watch."
> ³⁵And He went a little beyond them, and fell to the ground and began to pray that if it were possible, the hour might pass Him by.
> ³⁶And He was saying, "Abba! Father! All things are possible for You; remove this cup from Me; yet not what I will, but what You will."

So, if you pray for something specific and do not receive a miracle, rest assured that God is still in control. You are in good company. He allows trials to enter our lives for His purposes. We can pray, and even pray for good things, but we cannot demand God to perform miracles outside of His will. And yet, we are called to pray without ceasing anyway. God will reveal His will. Sometimes He chooses to allow a child to die, even His own child, Jesus Christ. C. S. Lewis, in his book of essays entitled *The World's Last Night And Other Essays*, expands on this issue:

> Prayer is not a machine. It is not magic. It is not advice offered to God. Our act, when we pray, must not, any more than all other acts, be separated from the continuous act of God himself, in which alone all finite causes operate.
>
> It would be even worse to think of those who get what they pray for as a sort of court favorites, people who have influence with the throne. The refused prayer of Christ in Gethsemane is answer enough to that. And I dare not leave out the hard saying which I once heard from an experienced Christian: "I have seen many striking answers to prayer, and more than one that I thought miraculous. But they usually come at the beginning: before conversion or soon after it. As the Christian life proceeds, they tend to be rarer. The refusal, too, are not only more frequent; they become more unmistakable, more emphatic."[1]

I would in no way want to propose that God works in miraculous ways on a regular basis, or as a matter of course. I would not say He does so in any effort to further validate what has already been captured on the pages of Scripture, or to offer some new form of revelation to mankind. Miracle workers and modern day faith healers are a dime a dozen, and most do their works for their own glory and not for God's glory. But, I do most certainly believe that God performs miracles in His church today. God responds to our prayers, and when it is His will to do so, He intervenes in time and space and works miracles.

Some scholars go on to say that the only thing you can truly consider a miracle is a sign that is performed in front of a large group of spectators. They say there are no such things as *private miracles*, and that God never works in miraculous ways outside of a very narrow definition: to provide explicit revelation to a large group of people. But, I disagree. That would be a convenient definition to move forward a particular theological perspective, but it just doesn't square with what is revealed in Scripture. God worked tons of *so-called private miracles*.

What do you say about Abraham offering up Isaac and a ram being provided for the sacrifice instead? That was a private experience between only two people, a father and his son. Or, what about the Angel of the Lord wrestling with Jacob and leaving him with a permanent limp as a reminder of his encounter? No one else benefitted from that miracle besides Jacob. How about Samson tearing apart an attacking lion with

---

1. Lewis, *The World's Last Night And Other Essays*, 10.

his bare hands, without any witnesses? What about Moses being amazed by a burning bush that was not consumed, while all alone pasturing his flocks? Philip was sent to preach the Gospel to the Ethiopian eunuch, and Peter was sent to preach to Cornelius, both private miracles. Paul was struck blind on the road to Damascus at his conversion, with only a few traveling companions. There are a lot of private miracles recorded in Scripture. God does not always choose to work miracles on a grand scale. Sometimes he communicates to very intimate groups or individuals with His miraculous power.

Some believe that God worked that way at a particular time in history, but relegate Him to a very mundane existence today. Or even worse, some believers have bought into secular philosophy and have had their belief in miracles *educated* out of them. They straddle the fence and try to blend a saving faith in Jesus, with a conformist acceptance that miracles are either unscientific or the relic of old-school Christianity. You can't have it both ways. Either it's truth or it isn't. They would not presume to request God to perform miracles in their ho-hum lives.

God recorded and preserved a testimony of how He has chosen to relate to mankind. Granted *not all the time*, but definitely *some of the time*, He chooses to command our undivided attention with miracles. He chooses to touch our lives and provide for our needs in awesome ways. There is no explanation for people who should have died, for the prosperity of the Gospel behind iron curtains, or for the orchestration of events that are utterly outside our control.

I think you would be hard-pressed to find a Christian missionary who has served on any foreign soil for any length of time, who would not attest to the miracles they had witnessed in that vocation. They know that Satan works differently in different parts of the world and have seen him hard at work. They also know that the Holy Spirit works differently there as well, and have seen Him hard at work performing miracles.

At this point we have to be careful. Satan uses miracles to deceive people as well. A Buddhist friend of mine told me stories of how she saw people actually levitated off the ground, and because of that *evidence* she chose to believe in her particular sect of Buddhism. Make no mistake, Satan does use counterfeit miracles to deceive. Again, if you don't believe me, ask a missionary to tell you what they have seen on the mission field. Remember that just because all Satan has to do in America is keep us fat and happy (as well as simply busy and distracted) doesn't mean he isn't working more overtly elsewhere. And, counterfeit miracles are part of that effort.

God does choose to astound us with His power, still today. The church age is not an era of silence, like the 400 years that passed between the testaments. The Holy Spirit is active in His church and God does respond to our prayers. When it is His will to do so, He chooses to work miracles.

THOUGHT QUESTIONS FOR CHAPTER 13

1. How would you define God's will?
2. Why is God's Glory so paramount to Him?
3. How might God be glorified in the way you walk through a difficult time?
4. Why are trials a part of God's will?
5. Can you think of other private miracles that God performed in the Bible? Has He performed any private miracles in your life?
6. What are some of the things that you are praying for without ceasing?

14

Pray Big!

I HOPE THIS BOOK has encouraged you to stand in awe of your mighty God. Hopefully, it has encouraged you to think through both the logical and Biblical reasons we believe in God and His miraculous power. Hopefully, it has helped you to solidify and put words to your belief in a creative, wonder-working God.

Hopefully, you have seen the error in the way several key passages have been handled, which has changed our evangelical view about the subject of praying for miracles. It seems to me that their interpretation and misinterpretation waters down our powerful God and the powerful lives we are called to live.

It seems that several misunderstood passages have led to faulty theology on the subject of miracles and have actually ham-strung our ability to pray as we ought to and experience the power of God in our daily lives. It has made our prayer life timid and weak. We are afraid to cross the line by even asking for God to work His miracles. It has not only changed the way we view God, but also the way we relate to Him.

Unfortunately, humanism seems to have crept into the church and made us tone down our awesome message, and has even embarrassed us into cowardice, and pushed the mute button on our bold testimony. Not wanting to be found testing, outright sinful or just immature, we have been stifled and have simply stopped asking, seeking and knocking as we have been instructed to do. We have ceased praying, rather than praying without ceasing.

It has long been my contention that the modern American church has diluted the bold message of Scripture and watered down the Gospel in an effort to fit in better with the current cultural landscape. It seems that the insidious disease of humanist philosophy has crept into our theology, our churches, and even, to some degree, our exposition of God's Word. That is why I spent so much time early on refuting those faulty systems that have invaded our ranks and effectively made us mute before our society, rather than bold in our defense of God and His miraculous Scriptures. May it never be!

So, in the words of some of the athletic coaches you may have heard in your life, I say, "Go big or go home!" How's that for a pep talk? Our message has always been and will always be at odds with the mainstream. The day we wake up and find that our train is rolling down the same tracks as the rest of our culture it is truly time for panic!

From creation to the times of the Patriarchs and the Prophets, to Christ's earthly ministry, and the early church, the dark and sinful hearts of people do not like being confronted by truth and light. They will naturally buck against it and do everything in their power to discredit it, in an attempt to get that annoying light out of their eyes. John 3:18–20 puts it this way:

> [18]He who believes in Him is not judged; he who does not believe has been judged already, because he has not believed in the name of the only begotten Son of God.
> [19]This is the judgment, that the Light has come into the world, and men loved the darkness rather than the Light, for their deeds were evil.
> [20]For everyone who does evil hates the Light, and does not come to the Light for fear that his deeds will be exposed.

Those of us fortunate enough to have been raised in America surrounded by religious freedom and tolerance have begun encountering an opposition to Christianity in ways that we have not known in our lifetime. We are beginning to experience some of the forceful oppression that used to be reserved for our brothers and sisters in other parts of the world, behind the iron curtain, or in other strongholds. The question is—will we stand?

Christianity is counter culture. We need to accept that and embrace it in order to be effective witnesses. It has implications for our evangelism and newly-formed church models. We don't have to make all of our churches look and feel so cozy and familiar, or so-called *seeker-sensitive* to the lost world. Truth is truth! The more it conforms to our lost culture the less it is truth! Our truth should stand in direct contrast to our secular culture, not actively seek to fit into it more comfortably, just like light is in contrast to darkness. Our churches, our message and even our worship style do not have to be more palatable to the lost. It is an acquired taste, that only true believers will grow to crave. We should look differently, smell differently, walk differently and talk differently than the lost world around us. We don't have to worry that the scientific community dismisses us and our belief in a miraculous Savior as uneducated buffoons. We shouldn't care if the Gospel is offensive to some who hear it. Christ Himself was called to be a rock of offense in 1 Peter 2:4–10:

> ⁴And coming to Him as to a living stone which has been rejected by men, but is choice and precious in the sight of God,
> ⁵you also, as living stones, are being built up as a spiritual house for a holy priesthood, to offer up spiritual sacrifices acceptable to God through Jesus Christ.
> ⁶For this is contained in Scripture: "Behold, I lay in Zion a choice stone, a precious cornerstone, and he who believes in Him will not be disappointed."
> ⁷This precious value, then, is for you who believe; but for those who disbelieve, "The stone which the builders rejected, this became the very cornerstone,"
> ⁸and, "*a stone of stumbling and a rock of offense*"; for they stumble because they are disobedient to the word, and to this doom they were also appointed.
> ⁹But you are a chosen race, a royal priesthood, a holy nation, a people for God's own possession, so that you may proclaim the excellencies of Him who has called you out of darkness into His marvelous light;
> ¹⁰for you once were not a people, but now you are the people of God; you had not received mercy, but now you have received mercy.

We don't have to be timid or even silent on the issue of miracles. God never has been! Scripture never has been! Our society needs to be confronted by truth, not cajoled by it. Sure, Jesus went where sinners went. But, he offered a clear alternative, and boldly confronted their sin and their need for a Savior. He wasn't trying to merely win friends, He was trying to win souls. That is what we should be about, too. We should go to them, but not just offer them more of the same, let's offer a clear alternative.

Praying for Miracles

We don't need to shine a dim flashlight with its warm and comfortable glow on those who are lost so as not to scare them away. We need to be a beacon shining a spotlight on their desperate need. In some ways, shock and awe are more effective tools of evangelism than the current seeker-sensitive model. I'm all for friendship evangelism, and the idea of winning the right to be heard. But, there has to come a time when we are bold enough with our new found friends to actually *be heard* and to speak the truth in love. It is okay to be bold and to pray big!

The Apostle Paul reminds us that miracles and our belief in the miraculous are precisely what sets us apart in I Corinthians 15:12-20:

> [12]Now if Christ is preached, that He has been raised from the dead, how do some among you say that there is no resurrection of the dead?
> [13]But if there is no resurrection of the dead, not even Christ has been raised;
> [14]and if Christ has not been raised, then our preaching is vain, your faith also is vain.
> [15]Moreover we are even found to be false witnesses of God, because we testified against God that He raised Christ, whom He did not raise, if in fact the dead are not raised.
> [16]For if the dead are not raised, not even Christ has been raised;
> [17]and if Christ has not been raised, your faith is worthless; you are still in your sins.
> [18]Then those also who have fallen asleep in Christ have perished.
> [19]If we have hoped in Christ in this life only, we are of all men most to be pitied.
> [20]But now Christ has been raised from the dead, the first fruits of those who are asleep.

If we have enough faith to believe in the resurrection of our Lord, why do we limit God in our personal lives? If He is powerful enough to provide for our salvation through the substitutionary death and miraculous resurrection of Jesus from the dead, then why do we live such timid lives? Paul boldly proclaims this fact in Romans 1:15-17:

> [15]So, for my part, I am eager to preach the gospel to you also who are in Rome.
> [16]For I am not ashamed of the gospel, for it is the power of God for salvation to everyone who believes, to the Jew first and also to the Greek.
> [17]For in it the righteousness of God is revealed from faith to faith; as it is written, "But the righteous man shall live by faith."

Can you say that? Or are you ashamed of the Gospel? Maybe just a little? Does it honestly depend on whom you are talking to? Among Christian friends you may be bold as a roaring lion, but what about when you are confronted by the sneering unbeliever, who dismisses you outright? Is your message the same all the time? Or does your courage wane when you face the sharp jabs of worldly folks who laugh at you to your face? Are you ashamed of the Gospel?

The pages of the Scripture, both the Old and New Testament, scream that He is a wonder-working God. He is the one who created everything, and the only one who can intervene in the order which He has created. Psalm 72:18–19 encourages:

> [18] Blessed be the Lord God, the God of Israel, who alone works wonders.
> [19] And blessed be His glorious name forever; and may the whole earth be filled with His glory Amen, and Amen.

During the triumphal entry of Jesus into Jerusalem, before He was crucified, we are taught to cry out boldly of His miracles. In Luke 19:37–40 we read:

> [37] As soon as He was approaching, near the descent of the Mount of Olives, the whole crowd of the disciples began to praise God joyfully with a loud voice for all the miracles which they had seen,
> [38] shouting: "Blessed is the king who comes in the name of the Lord; Peace in heaven and glory in the highest!"
> [39] Some of the Pharisees in the crowd said to Him, "Teacher, rebuke Your disciples."
> [40] But Jesus answered, "I tell you, if these become silent, the stones will cry out!"

My great fear is that our generation has been so influenced by political correctness and so shamed by the media, philosophers, and scientists, that we have become silent on the issue of miracles. Notice why the crowd during the Triumphal Entry was joyfully shouting. It was because of the miracles which they had seen! Maybe we have stopped shouting in the streets because we have never experienced miracles in our own lives. Perhaps you have no reason to shout. In that case, I cannot blame you for quietly sitting on your palm branch on the side of the street as Jesus passes by.

The modern day Christian church cannot be silent on the issue of miracles. Either God is God or He is not! Either we believe in our wonder working God or we don't. Jesus has a back-up plan, if we become silent, then His inanimate creation, even the rocks themselves, will rise up and take our place. Humbling isn't it?

You serve a big God! One of the keys and prerequisites to praying for miracles is having a right relationship with the one true God. Without a saving relationship to God through His only Son Jesus Christ, you are in the same position as the prophets of Baal that we explored earlier. You can rant and rave and put all your emotion into it, but no miracle will come. You have to be in right relationship to the only one who is capable of performing miracles.

Our view of God also has to grow, commensurate with His power to work miracles. In his classic theological work, *Knowing God*, J. I. Packer explores how far removed the modern church has become from understanding God's power and majesty:

> We are modern people, and modern people, though they cherish great thoughts of themselves, have as a rule small thoughts of God. When the person in the church, let alone the person on the street, uses the word God, the thought is rarely of divine *majesty*.
>
> A well-known book is called *Your God Is Too Small*; it is a timely title. We are poles apart from our evangelical forefathers at this point, even when we confess our faith in their words. When you start reading Luther, or Edwards, or Whitefield, though your doctrine may be theirs, you soon find yourself wondering whether you have any acquaintance at all with the God whom they knew so intimately.
>
> Today, vast stress is laid on the thought that God is *personal*, but this truth is so stated as to leave the impression that God is a person of the same sort as we are—weak, inadequate, ineffective, a little pathetic. But that is not the God of the Bible![1]

Another key to praying for miracles is your heart motivation. As we discussed at length, your faith can grow every time you witness God's enormous power, but only if you are praying with proper motives. And, don't forget God only works miracles if it is His will to do so. No man can conjure up the miracles of God if it is not first God's sovereign will to display them.

---

1. Packer, *Knowing God*, 83.

Pray Big!

How is your prayer life? That is a loaded question, as well as a convicting one to us all, myself included. If we believe what we say we believe, it will be reflected in our actions and in our prayer life. I want to conclude with one of my favorite passages in the Bible. Check out James 5:13–18:

> *[13]*Is anyone among you suffering? Then he must pray. Is anyone cheerful? He is to sing praises.
> *[14]*Is anyone among you sick? Then he must call for the elders of the church and they are to pray over him, anointing him with oil in the name of the Lord;
> *[15]*and the prayer offered in faith will restore the one who is sick, and the Lord will raise him up, and if he has committed sins, they will be forgiven him.
> *[16]*Therefore, confess your sins to one another, and pray for one another so that you may be healed. The effective prayer of a righteous man can accomplish much.
> *[17]*Elijah was a man with a nature like ours, and he prayed earnestly that it would not rain, and it did not rain on the earth for three years and six months.
> *[18]*Then he prayed again, and the sky poured rain and the earth produced its fruit.

I love that. Elijah was just a regular guy, not a super-saint. He prayed with a purpose. He wanted to show God for the miraculous, awe-inspiring God that He is. God was happy to oblige. Three and a half years passed without a single drop of rain. No El Nino, La Nina or global warming could explain that. Insurance adjusters still allow for the occurrence of the unexplainable in their profession, they call it *an act of God*. That is the only thing that could explain a phenomenon like the one described here. Then, Elijah prayed for God to send rain, and just like that . . . the skies opened and poured down rain.

It is one of my favorite passages in all of Scripture, "The effective prayer of a righteous man can accomplish much." All we are called to do is pray (without ceasing). God will decide if what we are praying for fits into His perfect will. Do you believe that? Then I challenge you to pray big! You will be amazed at what your miraculous God will do.

THOUGHT QUESTIONS FOR CHAPTER 14

1. Why are we, as Christians, called to go big or go home?
2. How is our belief in a wonder-working God counter-culture?
3. Why are miracles and God's awesome power something we need to shine a bright light on in our day and time?
4. How do God's miracles, those recorded in the Bible and witnessed in our life, make us bold?
5. What is your favorite miracle in the Bible? Why?
6. How is your prayer life? Are you bold enough to pray for big things of your big God?

Bibliography

Allies, Mary H. *Leaves from St. Augustine*. New York: Burns and Oates, 1886.

Aquinas, St. Thomas. *The "Summa Theologica" of Saint Thomas Aquinas*. New York: Benzinger Brothers, 1922.

Chafer, Lewis Sperry. *Systematic Theology*. Grand Rapids: Kregel Publications, 1993.

Dawkins, Richard. "The God Delusion T-Shirt." No pages. Online: http://store.richard dawkins.net/products/the-god-delusion-t-shirt.

Jefferson, Thomas. *The Life and Morals of Jesus of Nazareth: The Jefferson Bible*. New York: N.D. Thompson Publishing Co., 1902.

Kurtz, Paul. "Secular Humanist Manifesto 2000." No pages. Online: http://www.secular humanism.org. Retrieved 2011.

Lewis, C.S. *Miracles*. New York: Harper Collins, 2001.

Lewis, C.S. *The World's Last Night And Other Essays*. Orlando: Houghton Mifflin Harcourt, 1988.

Merriman-Webster Dictionary. "Religious." No pages. Online: http://www.merriam-webster.com/dictionary/religious.

Mueller, Rev. E. *Luther's Explanatory Notes on the Gospels*. York, PA: P. Anstadt and Sons, 1899.

Nidich, Susan. "Judges." In *The Oxford Bible Commentary*, edited by John Barton & John Muddiman, 182. Oxford: Oxford University Press, 2001.

Packer, J.I. *Knowing God*. Downers Grove IL. : Inter Varsity Press.

Ross, Hugh. "Why I Believe in Miracle of Divine Creation." In *Why I am a Christian*, edited by Norman L. Giesler and Paul K. Hoffman, 157. Grand Rapids: Baker Books, 2006.

Ryrie, Charles C. *So Great Salvation*. Wheaton, IL. : Victor Books, 1989.

Sagan, Carl. *Billions and Billions*. New York: Random House, 1998.

Swindoll, Charles. *Growing Strong in the Seasons of Life*. Grand Rapids: Zondervan, 1994.

Tozer, A. W. *I Call It Heresy!* Rockville, MD. : Wildside Press, 2010.

www.ingramcontent.com/pod-product-compliance
Lightning Source LLC
Chambersburg PA
CBHW072149160426

43197CB00012B/2310